EARLY CHILDHOOD EDUCATION SERIES

NANCY FILE & CHRISTOPHER P. BROWN, EDITORS

ADVISORY BOARD: Jie-Qi Chen, Cristina Gillanders, Jacqueline Jones,
Kristen M. Kemple, Candace R. Kuby, John Nimmo,
Amy Noelle Parks, Michelle Salazar Pérez, Andrew J. Stremmel, Valora Washington

To look for other titles in this series, visit www.tcpress.com

continued

Early Childhood Education Series, *continued*

We Are the Change We Seek

Advancing Racial Justice in Early Care and Education

Iheoma U. Iruka, Tonia R. Durden,
Kerry-Ann Escayg, and Stephanie M. Curenton

TEACHERS COLLEGE PRESS
TEACHERS COLLEGE | COLUMBIA UNIVERSITY
NEW YORK AND LONDON

Published by Teachers College Press,® 1234 Amsterdam Avenue, New York, NY 10027

Front cover photo by Weekend Images Inc. / iStock by Getty Images.

Library of Congress Cataloging-in-Publication Data

Names: Iruka, Iheoma U., author. | Durden, Tonia R., author. |
   Escayg, Kerry-Ann, author. | Curenton, Stephanie M., author.
Title: We are the change we seek : advancing racial justice in early care
   and education / Iheoma U. Iruka, Tonia R. Durden, Kerry-Ann Escayg,
   and Stephanie M. Curenton.
Description: New York, NY : Teachers College Press, [2023] |
   Series: Early childhood education series | Includes bibliographical
   references and index.
Identifiers: LCCN 2023004098 (print) | LCCN 2023004099 (ebook) |
   ISBN 9780807768020 (paperback) | ISBN 9780807768037 (hardcover) |
   ISBN 9780807781562 (ebook)
Subjects: LCSH: Early childhood education—Social aspects—United States. |
   Culturally relevant pedagogy—United States. | Racial justice in education—
   United States. | Discrimination in education—United States. | Educational
   equalization—United States.
Classification: LCC LB1139.25 .I78 2023 (print) | LCC LB1139.25 (ebook) |
   DDC 370.1170973—dc23/eng/20230315
LC record available at https://lccn.loc.gov/2023004098
LC ebook record available at https://lccn.loc.gov/2023004099

ISBN 978-0-8077-6802-0 (paper)
ISBN 978-0-8077-6803-7 (hardcover)
ISBN 978-0-8077-8156-2 (ebook)

Printed on acid-free paper
Manufactured in the United States of America

Contents

Acknowledgments

We are so grateful to our families and community who hold us down during this journey called life. We also want to acknowledge and recognize the countless children, families, educators, partners, colleagues, funders, editors, and most importantly our ancestors for giving us the will and the way to continue their fight for justice and freedom. The fact that four Black PhD women—who are mothers and caregivers, authors, scholars, social justice activists, and entrepreneurs—are writing their second book as a quartet testifies to all the shoulders we stand on and those we are learning and working beside. We speak and seek the truth and human dignity for all. As Malcolm X says in his The Ballot Or the Bullet speech in Cleveland, Ohio on April 3, 1964, *"Speaking like this doesn't mean that we're anti-white, but it does mean we're anti-exploitation, we're anti-degradation, we're anti-oppression."*

We Are the Change We Seek

Introduction

During the conception and writing of this book, a lot was happening in the United States and across the globe. The COVID-19 pandemic created havoc and loss in many people's lives, especially for Black, Latine, and Indigenous families and communities who were especially hit hard. Meanwhile, as many of us huddled at home, trying to stay safe from the virus, there was, seemingly, a daily onslaught of news reporting the murder of unarmed Black people like Ahmaud Arbery, Breonna Taylor, and the videotaped murder of George Floyd that rocked our country. The culmination of the emotional impact of COVID-19 and disparate effects coupled with these senseless murders have triggered attention to racism, especially anti-Black racism, and there were demonstrations and calls for policies and practices to dismantle inequitable systems.

More than two years have passed since these massive demonstrations and calls for addressing racism and structural inequities, such as unfettered police violence against Black communities and disparities in wealth and housing, and for ensuring access to high quality early education, political representation, and civil rights protections. Still, it is unclear whether there has truly been racial progress, especially as white supremacist organizations have methodically coalesced and organized, infiltrating political offices, corporations, news media, and educational institutions. The protests sparked by the murders of Black people also drew attention to the struggles of other marginalized groups from Asian American, Pacific Islanders, and Latine people to the LGBTQI+ community.

Nevertheless, we are encouraged that attention to racial equity is still a focus in many places nationally and locally, propelled in particular by the Biden Administration's Executive Order 13985 on Advancing Racial Equity and Support for Underserved Communities Through the Federal Government. For its part, impelled by a severe workforce shortage that started before the pandemic-era "great resignation" and was exacerbated during it, the early childhood field has raised more calls for improving the treatment and recognizing the value of early childhood educators, the majority of whom are women and also members of racially and ethnically minoritized groups.

These women have been asked to work during a pandemic that saw many shutter themselves from the world. They have received subpar wages for their heroic and brain-building efforts. Simultaneously, we know many Black, Latine, and Indigenous households and other households of color continue to suffer from the structural racism and discrimination that has hindered their social, health, and economic progress. Black children and other children of color continue to suffer the consequences of racism, bias, and bigotry, through the gaze and in the shackles of white supremacy. Black, Latine, and Indigenous children and other children from marginalized communities deserve peace, healing, and most importantly, love.

With all these challenges in mind, we offer ideas on how to move from gap-gazing to facing racism, a historical and present problem, in early childhood education (ECE). Using our culturally responsive, anti-bias, and anti-racist (CRABAR) approach, we suggest ways to bring anti-bias and anti-racist approaches to your teaching space, your assessment tools, and adequate compensation of early childhood educators. We provide the RICHER framework with its six elements as a way to activate the CRABAR approach by examining your teaching and your positionality, wherever you are in the ECE space.

We are so thrilled that you are reading this book, and hope that it meets you where you are on your racial equity journey and motivates you to do more than you thought possible to dismantle racism and all dehumanization in your space.

HOW TO USE THIS BOOK

The goal of this book is to stimulate action in the classroom, program, and community. It is for educators, clinicians, and those seeking to move forward in their racial equity journey to ensure equity for young children. This book can be used in multiple ways, from early childhood courses to book study groups. It can be read solo or with friends, colleagues, and community groups. For example, as many schools and programs develop book study groups, communities of practice, and speaker series focused on starting or strengthening their justice, equity, diversity, and inclusion priorities, this book can serve as a primary resource guide. Individuals, including teachers, coaches, trainers, administrators, can use this book to enhance their culturally responsive and anti-bias practices, examining areas for improvement, and building on areas of success.

Beyond reading the book, we encourage you to actively engage with the book and record your thoughts in a separate journal. We include many reflective questions and activities to stimulate your mind, body, and soul, and ask that you bring your whole self as you journey with this book. There is no right or wrong answer. The only wrong is not seeking to be the change we seek for our babies, families, and communities.

CHAPTER 1

Racism's Past, Present, and Future

Ever since the birth of our nation, white America has had a schizophrenic personality on the question of race—a self in which she proudly professed the great principles of democracy and a self in which she sadly practiced the antithesis of democracy. . . . The step backward has a new name today. It is called the white backlash.

—Martin Luther King, Jr., 1968

Social science research tells us that race is nothing more than an antiquated social construct, not an eternal, objective, genetic fact. Lopez (1995) notes that "Races are categories which exist only in society; they are produced by myriad conflicting social forces; they overlap and inform social categories; they are fluid rather than static or fixed; and they only make sense only in relationship to other racial categories" (p. 199). Nonetheless, race as an idea endures in popular thought and is "inextricably linked to European expansion and colonization" (Dei, 1996; Lopez; 1995; Davis & MacNaughton, 2009). It is a powerful concept in the United States and around the globe and shapes perceptions, social relations, and life experiences in countless ways. In this book we explore how racism manifests in different settings, from healthcare and policing to welfare and education. We also examine how racism impacts families of color across contexts. Together, this knowledge will help readers understand that to move toward a just society, we must know our history and go through the trials and tribulations of repair and healing. To provoke a broader understanding of these concepts from an individual perspective, we encourage readers to delve more deeply into the material in question by making meaningful connections to equitable principles, personally and professionally.

WHAT IS RACISM?

Race is a concept used to consolidate power; *racism* is the tool that uses that concept.

This tool has organized power, access, and resources around white people and whiteness while also oppressing, denigrating, and dehumanizing those who are not white. It operated in many ways to justify the enslavement of Africans. This tool means that white people, people who look white, or whiteness based on language and culture, benefit from this system and arrangement of power. Whiteness is regarded as beautiful, intelligent, worthy, and something to aspire to. This tool called racism is so powerful that it is hard to see; it is the air we breathe. It is part of our culture. Do you ever wonder why all but one of the "leaders of the free world" (i.e., U.S. presidents) has been a white male? We start with this definition, this question, because before we discuss racism's impact in early childhood, it is critical to understand how deeply racism is embedded in the roots of our country.

Early childhood education (ECE) is one of the many spaces that children experience that directly and indirectly impact their health, development, and well-being. While we focus on a few areas, we acknowledge that racism is in everything: media, housing, food access, business, and so much more. Understanding how other contexts, such as criminal justice, health care, and education, intersect with racism allows us to get a sense of all the systems and settings that have either already impacted families or will eventually touch our children, requiring ECE professionals to endow our babies with as much protection as possible as they traverse this world.

Racism and Police Violence

Why is it easy for police officers to gun down a Black youth who is doing everyday things but not harm an 18-year-old white shooter who killed 12 older Black people who were grocery shopping in a Buffalo, NY, supermarket? The answer lies in recognizing the "specificity of anti-blackness" (Dumas & Ross, 2016, p. 46). Specifically, the ideology of anti-Blackness is evidenced in the innumerable ways that Black bodies continue to be classified as nonhuman, which, in turn, sanctions collective and individual acts of physical and psychological violence toward Black people (Dancy et al., 2018; Husband & Escayg, 2022).

Racially motivated violence constitutes the culminating expression of anti-Blackness. For example, according to Mapping Police Violence, a nonprofit group that tracks police shootings, Black people account for 13% of the U.S. population, but accounted for 27% of those fatally shot and killed by police in 2021 (Mapping Police Violence, 2022). They find that Black people are 2.9 times more likely to be killed by police officers than are white people. For every 1 million people, 88 Pacific Islanders and 67 Black people are killed compared to 23 white people (see Figure 1.1).

Figure 1.1. Police killing in the United States per 1 million people by race and ethnicity, 2013–2022

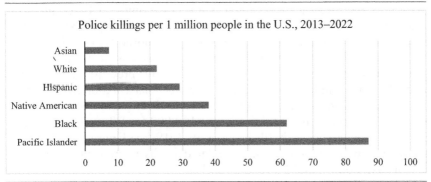

Source. From Mapping Police Violence (2022). https://mappingpoliceviolence.org/?year=2022&location=the+U.S.&race=people&chart=RateByRace

Figure 1.2. Racial/ethnic category of 4,467 victims of lynching, 1883–1941

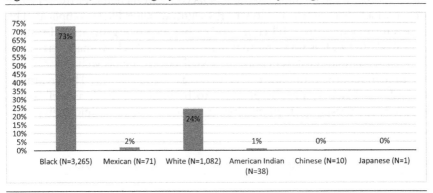

Source. Adapted from Seguin & Rigby (2019).

There is a similar racial disparity in lynching. According to the study by Seguin and Rigby (2019), the great preponderance of 4,467 total victims of lynching from 1883 to 1941 were Black men. 4,027 victims were men, 99 were women, and 341 were of unknown gender (although likely male); 3,265 were Black, 1,082 were white, 71 were Mexican or of Mexican descent, 38 were American Indian, ten were Chinese, and one was Japanese (see Figure 1.3). A thread connects the origin of policing, the antebellum slave patrols who monitored and punished enslaved Black people, to our current institution of policing that disproportionately physically and psychologically harms and incarcerates Black people with impunity (Brucato, 2020).

Racism and Healthcare

Why does the medical professional immediately ignore a Black pregnant mom who reports discharge or other concerns during pregnancy? Data show continuing racial disparities in maternal mortality, especially striking in the United States with a supposed world-class healthcare system. According to the Centers for Disease Control and Prevention, 40.8 Black and 29.7 American Indian/Alaska Native women per 100,000 live births die in connection with pregnancy, which is two to three (or more) times higher than the 12.7, 11.5, and 13.5 deaths per 100,000 for White, Hispanic, and Asian women, respectively (Petersen et al, 2019; see Figure 1.3). Evidence shows that many of these pregnancy-related deaths are preventable (Centers for Disease Control and Prevention, 2019).

These stark racial disparities are also seen in infants: 10.8 Black, 9.4 Native Hawaiian and Other Pacific Islander, and 8.2 American Indian/Alaska Native infants per 1,000 are likely to die in their first year of life compared to 3.6 for Asian, 4.6 for White, and 4.9 for Hispanic infants (Jang & Lee, 2022). Some of the birthing risk factors faced by women and birthing people of color include pre-term and low birthweight, which is likely complicated by access to prenatal care (Hill et al., 2022), but also intergenerational trauma (NASEM, 2019). It is no secret that many enslaved Black women were raped by their white male enslavers both for sexual satisfaction as well as for breeding to maintain the economic engine that was chattel slavery. This treatment of enslaved Black women as property to be bred and used, as well as the enslavers' ownership of their children to maintain the economic engine until

Figure 1.3. Pregnancy-related death rate by race/ethnicity, 2007–2016

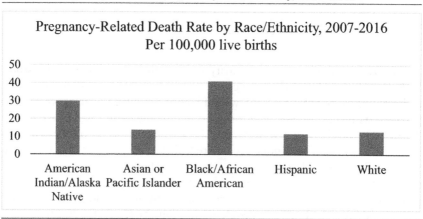

Source. From Petersen et al., 2019, p. 763.

they were no longer needed (Smithers, 2012), is visible in the maternal mortality statistics, but also in how Black children are seen and treated today.

Racism and School Discipline

Why are 36- and 49-month-old Black children being harshly punished and expelled from their preschools, most often for relatively benign behaviors? There is no evidence that Black children are predisposed to be more violent or oppositional behaviors than their white peers. However, there is a constant view of them as more mature and more likely to cause problems to which the response must be suspension or expulsion (Cooke et al., 2021). The "adultification" of Black children seems to persist alongside a conceptual obstinacy that excludes Black children from the traditional sanctification of children's—above all, white children's—unformed character as, in general, "innocent" (Burton, 2007; Davis & Marsh, 2020; Iruka & Hawkins, 2022). This view perpetuates racist social conventions, inequity, and is harmful and dehumanizes Black children even as their white counterparts embody consecrated archetypes and are the exclusive beneficiaries of the protection and safety associated with the concept of innocence (Escayg & Farago, in press; Goff et al., 2014). For instance, according to the 2017–2018 Civil Rights Data Collection of the Office for Civil Rights, Black preschool students accounted for 18.2% of total preschool enrollment but received 43.3% of out-of-school suspensions. Black preschool students were expelled at rates that were more than twice their share (38.2%) of total preschool enrollment (18.2%) (see Figure 1.4) (Office for Civil Rights, 2021). In addition, Black boys made up less than 10% of the enrollment (9.6%) but almost one out of three (30.4%) of expelled children, compared to white boys who made up nearly a quarter (23.8%) of enrollment but also almost a third of expelled children. This suggests that Black boys, who make a smaller percentage compared to white boys, are being overdisciplined.

Black girls' situation is similar to Black boys'. Black girls make up about 10% of preschool enrollment and almost one out of 10 (8%) expelled children, nearly double the rate for white girls at about 5% or one out of 20 expelled children. However, white girls make up almost 20% of enrollment, which is more than double the enrollment rate of Black girls (see Table 1.1).

Racism and Welfare Policies

Why are Mexican children separated from their parents at the border? Why are Native children removed from their families and placed in boarding schools and white homes to "Americanize" them? Why are Black children taken from their homes due to subjective determination of abuse and neglect? Whether it was taking away babies and children from Mexican families

Figure 1.4. Suspension and Expulsion among Preschool Children by Race/Ethnicity, 2017–2018

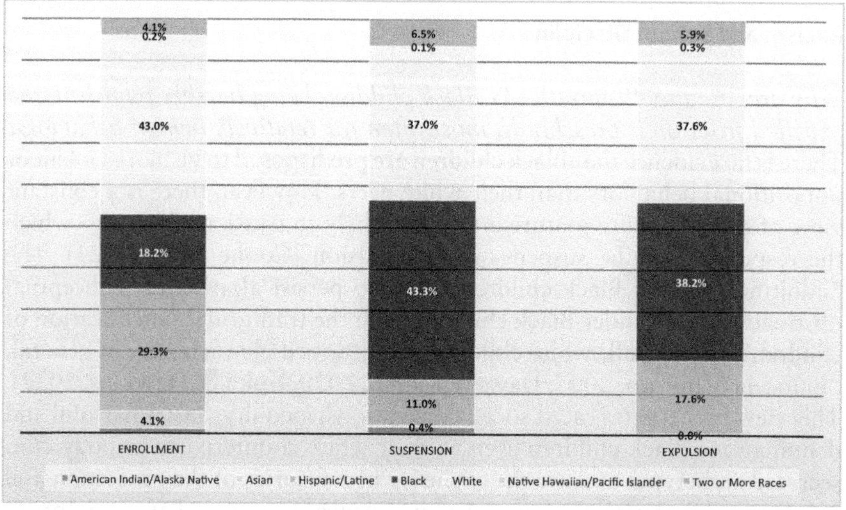

Source. U.S. Education Department, Office for Civil Rights. (2021, June). *Civil Rights Data Collection, 2017–18 State and National estimations: Discipline* (2021, June). https://ocrdata.ed.gov/estimations/2017-2018

crossing the southern U.S. border (de la Peña et al., 2019), the removal of Native American children from their homes and their placement in boarding schools or with white families to make them more acceptable and appealing to white people (Little & Hopkins, 2014), or the selling of enslaved Black children (Berry, 2017), the United States has a history of the traumatization, dehumanization, and separation of children of color from their families.

As with school discipline, we see disproportionality in Black children's involvement in the child welfare system. Black children make up about 14% of the child population but almost 23% of children in foster care (Kids Count Data Center, 2018) (see Figure 1.5). Similarly, American Indian/Alaska Native children are less than 1% of the population but make up almost 3% of children in foster care. In contrast, white children make up over 50% of the child population but make up less than half of the child welfare cases at 44%.

Cultural Racism

These examples of brutality, dehumanization, trauma, and oppression have been disproportionately used against Black, Native, Latine,[1] and other people of color. It does not mean that police do not wrongfully kill white people or that white mothers don't lose children during childbirth. It does

Table 1.1. Discipline of Preschool Students by Race/Ethnicity and Sex in 2017-18

	Boys			Girls		
	Enrollment	One or More Out-of-School Suspensions	Expulsions	Enrollment	One or More Out-of-School Suspensions	Expulsions
American Indian/Alaska Native	0.6%	1.6%	0.3%	0.5%	0.2%	0.0%
Asian	2.3%	0.4%	0.0%	1.8%	0.0%	0.0%
Hispanic/Latine	15.5%	9.5%	16.3%	13.8%	1.5%	1.3%
Black	9.6%	34.2%	30.4%	8.6%	9.1%	7.8%
White	23.8%	32.1%	33.0%	19.2%	4.9%	4.6%
Native Hawaiian/Pacific Islander	0.1%	0.0%	0.3%	0.1%	0.0%	0.0%
Two or More Races	2.2%	5.2%	4.6%	1.9%	1.3%	1.3%
Total	54.1%	83.1%	85.0%	45.9%	17.0%	15.0%

Source. U.S. Education Department, Office for Civil Rights, Civil Rights Data Collection, 2017–18 State and National Estimations (2021, June). https://ocrdata.ed.gov/estimations/2017-2018

Figure 1.5. Foster Care Placement by Race/Ethnicity, 2018

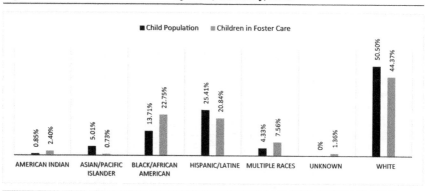

■ Child Population   ■ Children in Foster Care

	AMERICAN INDIAN	ASIAN/PACIFIC ISLANDER	BLACK/AFRICAN AMERICAN	HISPANIC/LATINE	MULTIPLE RACES	UNKNOWN	WHITE
Child Population	0.85%	5.01%	13.71%	25.41%	4.33%	0%	50.50%
Children in Foster Care	2.40%	0.73%	22.75%	20.84%	7.56%	1.36%	44.37%

Source. Adapted from Kids Count Data Center (2018).

not mean that white children are not suspended from school or taken away from families by child welfare authorities. However, the persistent racial disparities across economic lines are indicators of differential treatment, primarily because of one's race, skin color, or phenotype (i.e., how they look). This is what is called *cultural racism*. It is embedded in the fabric of our society.

> Even semantics have conspired to make that which is black seem ugly and degrading. . . . There are some 120 synonyms for "blackness" and at least 60 of them are offensive . . . such as "blot," "soot," "grime," "devil," and "foul." There are some 134 synonyms for "whiteness" and all are favorable, expressed in such words as "purity," "cleanliness," "chastity," and "innocence." (King, 1968, p. 42)

James M. Jones (1972) described *cultural racism* as an all-encompassing perspective on one group's innate supremacy over another, entrenched in people's ideological views, everyday behaviors, language, symbols, and media.

A well-intentioned person may claim they are not racist and that they don't engage in racist actions. What such a person misses or ignores is that racism operates outside of individual intentions. *Systemic racism*, also called *structural* racism, is codified in policies, practices, and rules in the social, economic, health, civic, and educational sectors. As stated by Harvard Professor Dr. Camara P. Jones, an American physician, epidemiologist, and anti-racism activist who specializes in the effects of racism and social inequalities on health, structural racism is "codified in our institutions of custom, practice, and law, so there need not be an identifiable perpetrator. Indeed, institutionalized racism is often evident as inaction in the face of need" (Jones, 2000, p. 1212). Structural racism is the "totality of ways in which societies foster racial discrimination, through mutually reinforcing

Figure 1.6. Examples of Structural Racism

Discrimination (schooling, housing, employment, criminal justice, health care)	Segregation (residential, economic, social, and psychological)	Concentrated poverty / disinvestment	Mass incarceration
Police violence	Wealth gap (inequitable access to land, home, and safety nets)	Inequitable access to political power (voting, holding public office)	Inequitable immigraiton policies

inequitable systems (in housing, education, employment, earnings, benefits, credit, media, health care, criminal justice, and so on) that in turn reinforce discriminatory beliefs, values, and distribution of resources, which together affect the risk of adverse health outcomes" (Bailey et al., 2017, p. 1454). Examples of structural racism can be seen in Figure 1.6.

THE EFFECTS OF RACISM IN THE UNITED STATES

How Racism Impacts Families of Color (The Redding Family Example)

Racism, while invisible to many, is threaded throughout our daily lives. In September 2017, Shannon Jordy and Hafizah Omar of Living Cities—a cross-sector incubator focused on accelerating the spread and adoption of solutions through a racial equity lens—produced an infographic that depicts how racism impacts the daily lives of people of color through the Redding family's life. We discuss this infographic to show how racism affects children and their families. (See the infographic at https://livingcities.org/resources/a -day-in-a-life-how-racism-impacts-families-of-color-infographic/.)

Racism is multidimensional, operates on various levels, and morphs over time. It can have a complex impact on children's and adults' health and well-being (NASEM, 2019). In Jordy and Omar's example, each member of the Redding family experiences different types of racism, sometimes one at a time and sometimes at the same time. This graphic shows different kinds of racism, such as structural/institutional racism and individual racism/implicit bias.

1. Structural racism is codified in policies, practices, and rules in the social, economic, health, civic, and educational sectors. Structural racism is further organized within policies, practices, and norms in various institutions and agencies (i.e., institutional racism).

These inequitable practices and policies are deeply rooted and interconnected within and across various systems to maintain racial hierarchy in social, political, and economic contexts (Bonilla-Silva, 2017). These policies disadvantage individuals and groups people primarily based on their racial identity (Jones, 2000; Jones, 1972).

2. Individual bias is also called interpersonal discrimination and relates to personal interactions characterized by microaggressions. *Implicit bias*, also known as unconscious bias, is a set of automatic and uncontrolled cognitive processes that affect our attitudes toward others. *Individual racism*, also known as interpersonal racism, is based on beliefs of the superiority of one racial group over another and produces behaviors that preserve racial power. Examples of individual racism that are primarily based on race include:

- Failing to offer Black people who come to health care clinics for pain relief the same medical interventions as white people.
- Assuming that someone who appears to be Latine does not know English or is undocumented.
- Police officers assuming the white person at a crime scene is the chief of police and the Black person is the criminal.

There are different forms of racism, and we must know what they are even when they are not directed at or directly impacting us because it helps us to disrupt it. For example, immigration policies may not impact the classrooms and children directly as curriculum but they have reverberating effects across communities and generations of children.

THE MANY FORMS OF RACISM

Over the past 50 years, there has been a more precise articulation of forms of racism beyond structural, institutional, and individual. For example, *internalized racism* is when a racially/ethnically minoritized person adopts negative feelings, values, ideology, and attitudes toward their own racial or ethnic group (Jones, 2000). Neblett (2019) makes a note of other forms of racism, including *vicarious racism*, which refers to indirect experiences of racist acts committed against one's racial group; *everyday racism*, such as microaggressions; *cyber racism*, which is online and digital racism; *symbolic/modern racism*, which consists of negative beliefs or stereotypes about one's racial groups, and *aversive/implicit/contemporary racism*, which is the avoidance of particular racial groups. These various forms of racism operate and morph unpredictably through different institutions and individuals (Anderson et al., 2021).

Health care. Health care is viewed as foundational to good health. In our example, the mother, Patricia Redding, is likely to die prematurely; she has little access to quality care (likely due to living in a lower-quality neighborhood with few resources and services), and is the target of purveyors of health-harming substances (e.g., cigarettes, sugar-sweetened beverages) (Bailey et al., 2017). *This is an example of structural/institutional racism.* However, there is also bias in the health care field that provides lower-quality care for Black women, which leads to higher mortality compared to white women, such as not providing pain relief when requested and necessary (Hoffman et al., 2016). In this same study, the authors found that over a quarter of medical residents were likely to endorse the statement that "Black skin is thicker than whites'" and "Blacks have denser, stronger bones than whites." *This is an example of interpersonal/implicit bias.*

Transportation. Another part of daily life is transportation. The father, Darrell Redding, is likely to have transportation challenges. Data indicates that in addition to being less likely to have their own cars (Gautier & Zenou, 2010), Black, Latine, and Asian workers have longer commute times, leading to high transportation and even child care costs, as well as job instability (Parks, 2016). About 18% of Black households are without a vehicle compared to 6% of white households (see Figure 1.7). *This is an example of structural/institutional racism.*

Figure 1.7. Percent of U.S. Households Without a Vehicle by Race/Ethnicity, 2019

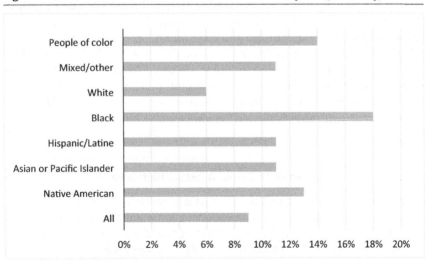

Source: National Equity Atlas. (n.d.). https://nationalequityatlas.org/indicators/Car_access#/

Education Opportunities. Black children are likely to be in an out-of-home care environment as early as six months old, whether in child care, preschool, or formal school. Black children like Tyrell and Faith Redding are less likely than white peers to have high-quality education opportunities. Data shows that Black children, regardless of family economic background, are likely to attend high-poverty schools, which also means they will not have the educational materials for learning, be in a healthy and safe environment, and be taught by certified and well-trained and compensated teachers (Gardner-Neblett et al., 2021). A report from EdBuild (2019) shows a $23 billion funding gap for school districts serving Black and Latine students compared to districts enrolling a comparable number of white students. This disparity in resources between predominantly Black and white schools is not surprising to anyone familiar with how public education is financed in this country; that is, primarily through property taxes.

Based on a legacy of Jim Crow laws and redlining, property taxes generate far less revenue in Black-majority communities, ultimately leading to educational disparities (Black & Crolley, 2022). *This is an example of structural/institutional racism.* Tyrell and Faith Redding also have a higher chance of being suspended and expelled than their white peers, which sets them up for the preschool to prison pipeline (Bacher-Hicks et al., 2021; Rashid, 2009). *This is an example of interpersonal/implicit bias.*

Economic Stability. Many jobs require higher education, from an associate degree to a professional degree. Even when federal assistance like the G.I. Bill was provided for war veterans, Black war veterans, like Grandpop Will, were systematically denied access to education and wealth-building, such as through homeownership (Katznelson & Mettler, 2008), which had a downstream impact on their earnings and their family's economic and social stability and well-being. In addition to inequitable access to higher education, Black people and other people of color are more likely than white people to have higher education loans and to default on those loans, which has a long-term impact on their economic stability (Addo et al., 2016). *This is an example of structural/institutional racism* (see text box).

STUDENT DEBT CRISIS: A RACIAL JUSTICE ISSUE

Considering all of the attention being paid to canceling student debt, one can argue that this is not just an economic issue but also a racial justice issue. It is hard on early childhood caregivers and educators, considering that the average pay for child care workers across all settings is $11.46 per hour, and it is the second lowest-ranked occupation by pay (McLean et al.,

2021). The Center for American Progress found that "On average, African American female teachers working full time make 84 cents for every $1 earned by their white counterparts. This 16 percent wage gap means a Black teacher would make $366 less per month and $4,395 less per year, on average" (Ullrich et al., 2016, p.1).

In the 2018 Early Childhood Workforce Index prepared for the Center for the Study of Child Care Employment (Whitebook et al., 2018), authors found that center-based Black early educators are more likely to earn less than $15 per hour than all other racial/ethnic groups in the early education workforce nationwide. Even after controlling for educational attainment, Black workers still earn lower wages than white workers ($.78 less per hour, or $1,622.40 less per year, for a full-time, full-year worker) (Whitebook et al., p.27). It is not, then, surprising that people of color have to take out more educational loans than other workers or that they are more likely to default, pay more of their incomes toward loan payments, and owe more than they borrowed (Scott-Clayton & Li, 2016).

In their analyses of the U.S. Department of Education Department of Education's Baccalaureate and Beyond (B&B) 93/97 and 08/12 surveys, which follow graduates from the 1993 and 2008 cohorts through 1997 and 2012, Scott-Clayton and Li (2016) found that racial disparities in student debt are much larger than thought and they have grown over the decades:

- In 2007–08, Black students had over $50,000 in student loans compared to $30,000 for Hispanics and less than $30,000 for Asians and whites. The student loans for Black students increased by more than $40,000 between 1992–93 and 2007–08.
- Black and Hispanic borrowers are likely to default compared to Asian and white borrowers, though this number dropped between 1992–93 and 2007–08.
- Black borrowers pay more than 20% of their income for their student loans compared to less than 15% for other borrowers, with this percentage significantly increasing for all borrows between 1992–93 and 2007–08.
- In 2007–08, almost 50% of Black Borrowers owe more after graduation than they borrowed compared to 23% for Hispanics and 10% for Asian and white borrowers.

Employment. Employment is the one way to move toward economic stability and upward mobility; however, Black and Latine people, especially males ages 18–33, like Tyrell Redding, are more likely to be unemployed than their white peers (Rodgers, 2022). For example, even now in 2022, when the overall unemployment rate is 3.6%, the unemployment rates for

Black men and women without a college education are 14.7% and 17.2%. In the first quarter of 2022, the unemployment rate for white workers was 3.0%, compared to 6.5% for Black workers, 4.6% for Hispanic workers, and 3.4% for Asian American and Pacific Islander workers (Economic Policy Institute, 2022). *This is an example of structural/institutional racism.* There are many reasons for racial disparities in unemployment, with some studies showing that "white-sounding names" are likely to get a call back for interviews compared to "Black-sounding names," such as Tyrell Redding or Darnell Redding vs. Heather or Sally Smith (Pager & Western, 2012). *This is an example of individual/implicit bias.*

Housing. One's home is supposed to be a place of safety, protection, and releasing of daily and life stressors, and for those who own homes, a way of building wealth. Unfortunately, there are racial disparities in housing, with about 43% of Black families owning homes compared to 50% of Latine families and over 75% of white families (Asante-Muhammad et al., 2021). The homeownership percentage for Black families today is similar to what it was in the 1960s. *This is an example of structural racism* (see text box). There are multiple reasons for these racial disparities in housing, including decades of redlining, devaluation of Black-owned properties, inequitable access to low-rate mortgages, which are *evidence of structural/institutional racism*, as well as the biases of loan officers and realtors that affect their choice of loan recipients and the homes they show to prospective buyers, which are examples of *individual/implicit bias* (Ray et al., 2021).

COMPOUNDING IMPACT OF HOUSING SEGREGATION

Structural segregation affected neighborhoods through *redlining,* by which Black communities were marked on maps with a literal red line by the Federal government: anyone who lived or bought property there would not be able to access federally backed loans. This means that Black people and those who lived in Black communities could not get these low-rate loans that made homeownership more affordable. Many Black people had to overpay or have multiple families living in one house. Housing segregation also led to de facto school segregation. As many school districts operated on a community-based model where children went to school in their community, Black children and those living in poor communities were relegated to low-resourced schools. In the landmark 1896 U.S. Supreme Court decision *Plessy v. Ferguson,* the Court said it was constitutional to have "separate but equal" facilities, and that segregated schools did not violate the Fourteenth Amendment of the Constitution about equal protection.

Black people sought different ways to provide education for their children, but the resources they could assemble could not match the long lineage of federal, state, and local resources provided to educate white children. Even when the "separate but equal" doctrine was dismantled in 1954 with the decision in *Brown v. Board of Education,* it took over 15 years to see an appreciable percentage of Black students attending schools where at least 50% of the children were white (Orfield et al., 2014).

Environmental Toxins. Even the air we breathe is racist, with extensive evidence showing that communities with a large proportion of Black people, such as the Reddings, face environmental toxins such as placement of factories and material run-off (Mikati et al., 2018; Richmond-Bryant et al., 2020). Data shows that many public housing projects, primarily built for Black people, used lead paint and lead pipes. Once ingested, there is no cure for lead poisoning, which impacts cognitive and social-emotional ability and regulation (Cassidy-Bushrow et al., 2017; Leech et al., 2016; Sampson & Winter, 2016). *This is an example of institutional/structural racism.*

Criminal Justice. Racial disparities in the criminal justice system are not new, with more Black and Latine people, especially males like 19-year-old Tyrell Redding, likely to be incarcerated at least once in their lifetime compared to white people (see Figure 1.8). The criminal justice system, and especially policing, has its origin in the Slave Patrols, whose mission was to "establish a system of terror and squash [enslaved person] uprisings with the capacity to pursue, apprehend, and return runaway [enslaved people] to their owners. Tactics included the use of excessive force to control and produce desired slave behavior" (NAACP, n.d.).

Figure 1.8. Average Rate of Black, Latine, and White Imprisonment per 100,000 Residents

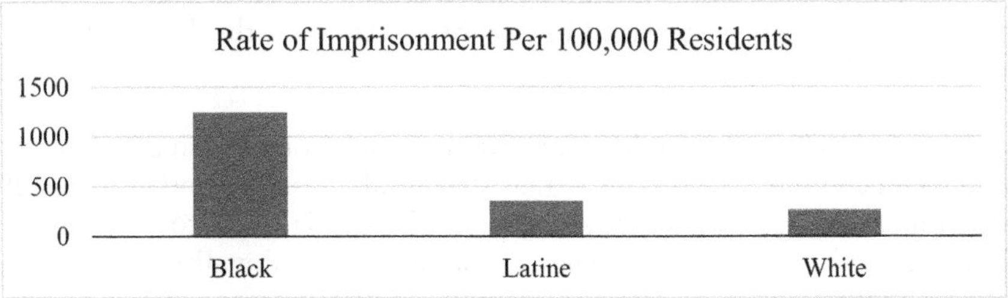

Source. From Nellis et al., 2021, p. 6.

Today we have a disproportionate rate of imprisoning Black and Latine people, especially Black males (Kovera, 2019). The top states that disproportionately imprison Black people compared to white people are New Jersey (Black people are 12.5 times more likely to be incarcerated than white people), Wisconsin (11.9%), Minnesota (9.7%), Connecticut (9.7%), and Maine (9.7%) (Nellis et al., 2021). (Wisconsin incarcerates 1 in 36 Black residents, compared to 1 in 214 for Massachusetts.) Several states also disproportionately imprison Latine people, including Arizona, Idaho, Wyoming, Connecticut, and Colorado.

AN INTERSECTIONALITY LENS

These are just a few examples of how racism impacts the daily lives of families of color. There are many more, such as workplace opportunities, pay, and interactions; bias when traveling, shopping, dining, partying, or engaging in everyday activities (e.g., resting in the dorm room, playing with a toy gun, waiting at a Starbucks for friends); interactions with police officers, school personnel, and other human service workers; and so much more. The Redding family's infographic shows us the interactions and compounding nature of structural racism and implicit bias and how they work in concert to maintain racial inequalities and a sense of being the "other" and perpetually in a state of fear and anxiety. However, we must understand that there is not one kind of experience, as families of color have a wide range of racial and ethnic backgrounds (e.g., Latine, Native American, Asian, multiracial) and are vulnerable to bias along many axes, including:

- Phenotype (i.e., skin color—colorism—or other aspects of appearance)
- Language (including whether they speak African American English)
- Where they live (including the region of the country and whether they live in an urban, suburban, or rural community)
- Socioeconomic level (i.e., income, education, wealth)
- Immigration status (including whether they are American Descendants of Enslaved People, first, second, or third generation, or mixed status)

Also, consider whether individuals are same-sex couples, single parents, and so much more. We recognize that structural racism and other forms of discrimination and bias work along more than racial lines to affect families and children. This lens is what we call an **intersectionality** lens. An intersectionality lens is essential to examine how a person experiences the world because of their racial category alongside other identities, such as their gender, language, economic levels, where they live, and so much more.

The Connection Between Structural Racism and Bias

"Why show this data and information about structural racism and its forms?"

"Why do we have to continue talking about the attempted eradication of the Native people and theft of their land, the enslavement and continued oppression of Black people, the imprisonment of Japanese people, the land seizure of Mexicans, and so much more?"

"What does addressing structural racism mean for addressing bias when I am only an early childhood teacher, assistant, or staff?"

These are just some of the questions often asked when discussing anti-bias practices in the classroom and programs serving young children. We can't discuss anti-bias practices in classrooms without discussing structural racism and other forms of racism such as interpersonal racism, internalized racism, and vicarious racism, to name a few. This lens was emphasized by Kathleen Osta and Hugh Vasquez of the National Equity Project (NEP) in their June 2019 essay entitled *Don't Talk About Implicit Bias Without Talking About Structural Racism*. Using the NEP framework linking structural racism and implicit bias (see Figure 1.9), we must first understand that racism is a white supremacy tool created to justify the enslavement, brutal treatment, and oppression of Black people, especially as a way to maintain chattel slavery as an economic engine of the country.

Through racism, policies and practices were codified that sought to preserve power and privilege for white people at the expense of Black people and other people of color. This codification of power through education, health, housing, criminal justice, voting, immigration policies, etc., ensured disparities for Black people and other people of color in education, health, wealth, political representation, housing, criminal justice, and so much more. These racist policies and practices ensured that when compared to white people and communities, Black people and other people of color score lower on all metrics.

For example, Black children are always shown as having lower cognitive abilities than their white peers based on reading, math, and science scores: the so-called achievement gap (de Brey et al., 2019). This achievement gap between Black (and other students of color) and white (and, more recently, Asian) students has been a focus of many reports, studies, interventions, and federal, state, and local priorities, which continues to maintain the narrative of Black children and other children of color being cognitively

Figure 1.9. The Link Between Structural Racism and Implicit Bias

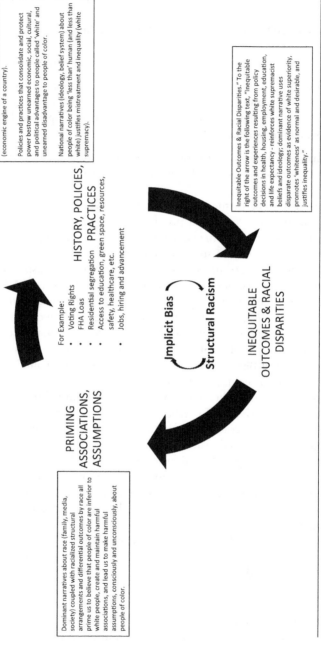

PRIMING ASSOCIATIONS, ASSUMPTIONS

HISTORY, POLICIES, PRACTICES

For Example:
- Voting Rights
- FHA Loas
- Residential segregation
- Access to education, green space, resources, safety, healthcare, etc.
- Jobs, hiring and advancement

Implicit Bias

Structural Racism

INEQUITABLE OUTCOMES & RACIAL DISPARITIES

Dominant narratives about race (family, media, society) coupled with racialized structural arrangements and differential outcomes by race all prime us to believe that people of color are inferior to white people, create and maintain harmful associations, and lead us to make harmful assumptions, consciously and unconsciously, about people of color.

Race is created to justify enslaving people from Africa (economic engine of a country).

Policies and practices that consolidate and protect power bestow unearned economic, social, cultural, and political advantages to people called 'white' and unearned disadvantage to people of color.

National narratives (ideology, belief system) about people of color being 'less than' human (and less than white) justifies mistreatment and inequality (white supremacy).

Inequitable Outcomes & Racial Disparities." "To the right of the arrow is the following text, "Inequitable outcomes and experiences resulting from policy decisions in health, housing, employment, education, and life expectancy - reinforces white supremacist beliefs and ideology; dominant narrative uses disparate outcomes as evidence of white superiority, promotes 'whiteness' as normal and desirable, and justifies inequality."

Source. From "Implicit Bias and Structural Racialization," by K. Osta & H. Vasquez, National Equity Project, 2019.

deficient and in need of "fixing." This continued narrative of the achievement gap and the inferiority of Black and brown people creates a priming effect. **Priming** is a psychological phenomenon in which a word, image, sound, or any other stimulus is used to elicit an associated response (Osta & Vasquez, 2019). So when people think about cognitive prowess, there is the assumption that white children are more intelligent than Black children and other children of color. This priming results in the assumption of superiority and association of brilliance and whiteness that is reified by providing more enriching educational opportunities like gifted and talented programs to white children compared to Black and Latine children, and the tracking of Black and Latine children into less enriching and special education programs compared to their white peers (Meek et al., 2020), which then results in maintaining the educational achievement gap.

This structural racism-to-implicit bias cycle started with structured inequities based on racism (in the United States, primarily related to skin color), which led to racial disparities in access and outcomes, followed by priming and association of deficit and race, leading to maintenance of and creation of racist policies based on biases (so the cycle continues). As an early childhood educator or professional—including those who work with educators, families, and community members; leaders or staff of a federal, state, or local organization, institution, or agency; or policymakers— the big question is, **what can you do to stop this perpetual cycle of racism?** This is where culturally relevant, anti-bias, and anti-racist practices/policies (CRABAR) come into play, which we discuss further in the following chapters of this book.

NOW WHAT?

We have provided a lot of information and data about how racism is in the air we breathe and is embedded in our policies and everyday actions. While some may think that racism is just a thing from the past, we can see it is harmful and, at times, has deadly consequences. The extent of racism can feel overwhelming because we may not be the doctors in charge of hospital practices, we are not a superintendent or on a school board, and may not even be a police officer, judge, or a lawyer who determines whether a crime has been committed and the punishment. However, everyone has a role to play in shifting how we treat people. There are many steps one can take toward change, including reading, engaging with diverse communities, and talking with families. Another step is to take your "bias temperature." Are you aware of the implicit biases in your attitudes toward groups of people based on race, religion, or sexuality? Everyone has biases; a first step toward managing yours is to become aware of them.

EDUCATORS' CORNER

Take the Implicit Attitudes Test

- Go to the Project Implicit site: https://implicit.harvard.edu/implicit/takeatest.html
- Take one of the computerized tests on this site. These take less than 5 minutes. We recommend you take the Race IAT but you can take many others, including the Sexuality, Religion, Skintone, and Disability tests.
- After taking it and getting your assessment results, journal for 5 minutes.

Here are some questions to ask yourself as you journal:

- Are you surprised by the results of your assessment? Why or why not?
- What were your emotions like before and after you took this assessment?
- What does this assessment result tell you about your perspectives and implications for your behaviors and practices?
- Can you identify how structural racism and other forms of racism are linked to your bias? Describe one thread that may contribute to your bias, such as education, poverty, criminal justice, and health.
- Optional: If you are doing this alone, feel free to journal about your bias for 5 minutes each day for the next week and keep track of how aware you are of your biases. If you are doing this in a group, feel free to share it with your group.

NOTE

1. Consistent with experts in the field, we use *Latine*, a gender-inclusive term commonly used throughout Spanish-speaking Latin America, to refer to individuals whose cultural background originated there. This is in place of using *Latinx*, a term Spanish speakers find unpronounceable in Spanish.

CHAPTER 2

Connecting Culturally Responsive, Anti-Bias, and Anti-Racist (CRABAR) Practices

> Meet Sam. Sam's aggressive behavior has been a challenge for the
> past month. Just yesterday, Sam kicked and injured a classmate on the
> playground, and unfortunately, these types of incidents have become more
> frequent. Sam's teacher, Arlene, feels as though the problem is that Sam
> hasn't been told at home that this is not acceptable behavior, and therefore
> doesn't know any better, so she dismisses Sam's behavior and hopes that
> it will get better soon.

What are the images of Sam that came to your mind? Is Sam a boy or girl? How old is Sam? What is Sam's race? What languages does Sam speak? What is the socioeconomic status of Sam's family? Who are the members in Sam's family? When a group of teachers were posed these questions they identified Sam as a Black boy from a lower-income family who is likely living with his mother, grandmother, and siblings. What came to mind when you envisioned Sam? To be equitable in our interactions and engagement with young children is to have the will and understanding of when we are not equitable—even in our thoughts and immediate images of children—like in the case of Sam.

Inequity *in action* usually manifests from the prejudices, stereotypes, and biases that we hold about ourselves and others. A *prejudice* is an opinion or belief about someone that we hold without specific knowledge. A *stereotype* is a widely held view about a particular type of person that is often what individuals use as justification for their prejudice. Lastly, the term *bias* as a noun represents our prejudices that are in favor of or against a group of people, and as a verb is when we *show* our preference or prejudice for or against someone.

As you recall from Chapter 1, we discussed the cycle between structural racism and bias. Prejudices and stereotypes are also maintained through the structural racism and bias cycle. Through the ideology of white supremacy that one race is superior to other races, policies and practices are created to confirm these belief systems. This ideology creates and reinforces negative views about individuals who are not part of the mainstream White cultural group. The unfortunate part is that these biases and stereotypes maintain an environment of unearned advantages to, for example, white people, men, higher income people, English speakers, and able-bodied individuals. Whereas Black, Indigenous, people of color, women, those living in poverty, bi-/multilingual speakers, and those with disabilities are provided with low or substandard opportunities and experiences including in early childhood education.

The biases that we *all* bring to our work in early childhood inevitably lead to actions and interactions with some children and families that unfortunately perpetuate the -isms we see in society: racism, sexism, ageism, classism, ableism, and other forms of bias. Racially and ethnically minoritized (REM) learners are disproportionately impacted by -isms in the early childhood classroom and beyond (Gilliam et al., 2016; Hilliard, 1997). In this chapter we explore an equity-centered framework that not only addresses racial educational disparities in early childhood education but also promotes cultural and academic excellence and healing.

ANTI-RACISM AND ANTI-BIAS

When you hear the word *anti-racism*, what do you think? When you hear the word *anti-bias*, what do you think? Let me ask the question differently. When you hear the word *anti-racism*, how do you *feel*? Also, pause to consider: Why do you feel this way? When you hear the word *anti-bias*, how do you feel? For more than 20 years, in our work as educators, scholars, researchers, and community advocates, we all have focused on introducing anti-bias and anti-racist concepts to educational leaders and educators. From this experience, we know that learning about and becoming an anti-racist and anti-bias teacher, scholar, or leader is just as much a *social–emotional experience* for the individual as it is a professional growth and development opportunity. Therefore, take a moment before moving forward with this chapter and first sit with these two words.

When you hear these terms, what are your immediate reactions and the thoughts, feelings and experiences that come to mind? What do they prompt you to do and learn more about? Do you question their appropriateness or relevance in early childhood education? Are you exhausted with or angered by the rhetoric you hear among those using these terms? Do you feel educators and leaders are all talk but no action related to concrete solutions in addressing bias and racism in early childhood education? It is important to first be clear on your position, knowledge, and understanding of the terms *anti-racism* and *anti-bias* before proceeding further in this book. We encourage you to lean into the moments in this chapter and beyond where you may question, cheer, or ponder the concepts, ideas, and strategies presented on the CRABAR framework we declare to be central to creating equitable educational experiences for Black and brown children.

TERMINOLOGY MATTERS: DEFINING BIAS AND RACISM

Now that you have critically reflected on your own emotional connection with these terms, let's further contextualize the terms *bias* and *racism*. We must have a basic understanding of bias and racism before we can understand how to create anti-bias and anti-racist experiences for young children. In simple terms, bias refers to our prejudice in favor of or against one person, group, or thing compared to another, usually in a way that is considered unfair. An example would be an early learning program leader's bias toward children who speak English fluently and clearly. This preference would then lead to an unfair and inequitable bias against a child or group of children, which might manifest as offering English-only programs and educational support strategies. It is important to emphasize that when there is negative inequity for one group of children, this creates privilege and a positive bias experience for other groups of children. So, for example, a favorable bias toward children who are standard English speakers leads to a curriculum, teacher competency, and family engagement that is centered around standard English modes of communication. Some people believe this is a great example of culturally grounded practices that then result in academic success and excellence. However, when we consider racial educational disparities in early childhood education, these culturally grounded practices benefit primarily native standard English speakers (Hilliard, 1997, 2003; S. King, 2020).

Let us be more explicit on how this example of bias is inequitable within the context of educating Black and brown children. Typically, racially and ethnically marginalized children's native language is not standard American English, but rather a complex combination of racial, cultural, and ancestral dialects they bring with them to the classroom (Gardner-Neblett et al., 2012; King, 2020). Because standard American English is the cornerstone of our early childhood educational system, the diverse languages and ways of speaking and communicating children bring to the classroom are not used as the foundational framework for instructional practices, which leads to experiences that are not culturally relevant and also, in some cases, children being misdiagnosed with speech sound disorders, learning disorders, or behavioral disabilities (Macrae et al., 2022). A positive bias toward children who speak standard English contributes to educational experiences that become inequitable for REM children.

Now, let's talk about race and racism. As mentioned previously in this book, we define race as a social construct in American society that has privileged or oppressed cultural groups based on skin color. *Racism,* a form of *negative bias*, refers to antagonism, discrimination, and prejudice directed against a person or people based on their membership in a particular racial or ethnic group. For example, a common negative bias that is a racist belief is that Black boys are unable to sit still; they are disruptive, lack self-control, and are overly aggressive (Essien, 2017). This bias and racist belief then leads to an action that is racist and inequitable. One example documented by research and our own anecdotal personal experience is the disproportionate number of Black and brown children impacted by preschool suspensions, expulsion, and early tracking into special education (Wymer et al., 2022). Unfortunately, there are policies, curriculum, and teaching practices that position young, REM learners in systems of educational inequity and oppression. The educational reality of REM learners impacted by racism in the early childhood classroom deserves more than a brief statement acknowledging its systemic existence within early childhood education. Therefore, let's dig a little deeper into the manifestations of bias and racism toward REM learners in early childhood.

RACISM IN EARLY CHILDHOOD EDUCATION

Let's start with experiences of Black children. As early as preschool, Black children are positioned within inequitable learning experiences through the documented high rates of preschool suspensions, early behavioral or learning disability labels, early psychological and educational impact of teacher/school racial bias, and the adultification of young Black girls and boys. Researchers have documented implicit and explicit bias and racism by teachers toward Black children as one explanation for the inequities imposed on Black children (Gilliam et al., 2016; Hilliard, 2003). Such inequities follow Black children throughout their educational trajectory and have long term impacts. For example, when we analyze early childhood outcome data based on race, we find there is a disproportionately high number of Black children in special education and disproportionately low number of Black children in advanced courses and gifted programs (Peters et al.,

2021). Furthermore, since the inception of popular theories such as culturally relevant pedagogy (Ladson-Billings, 1994 2014) and anti-bias education (Derman-Sparks, 1989; Derman-Sparks et al., 2020), when we look at 30-year educational trends (1990–2017) we find no significant change in reading and mathematics achievement (Musu-Gillette, De Brey, McFarland, Hussar, Sonneberg, & Wilkinson-Flicker, 2017). Therefore, we must ask ourselves whether we have truly moved beyond the rhetoric of culturally relevant, anti-bias, and equity-centered education to really focus on the complete integration of these concepts, beliefs, and teaching in every fabric of our early childhood educational system: teaching, learning, assessment, policy, teacher, and program quality.

INTRODUCING THE CRABAR FRAMEWORK

Our framework combines three seminal educational frameworks, which we will outline briefly in Table 2.1.

It is our stance that to create equitable learning experiences for Black and brown children, we need to *combine* the primary tenets of all three of these frameworks.

Culturally Relevant Pedagogy (CRP) provides a foundational guideline for teaching REM learners. A CRP approach provides the what and how of instruction and interaction with and for REM learners and their families. We draw upon this framework to provide a lens for teachers and teaching.

An anti-bias lens requires professionals to be intentional in their implementation of creating culturally relevant experiences for children. *Anti-bias education* requires teachers to constantly reflect on their own biases and -isms that they bring to the classroom while also explicitly and intentionally implementing interactions and curriculum that teach *children* to be anti-bias, fair, and equitable, and that inform them about the social inequities in our world. It is our position and experience that a teacher could teach in a culturally relevant manner, but not explicitly teach children about, or provide a curriculum centered on, *equity, justice, and fairness*.

Lastly, the anti-racist approach provides a very specific lens and positionality around the role and impact of racism, oppression and white privilege in early childhood. Escayg (2018, 2019) emphasizes how *anti-racist education* more readily promotes equity because it specifically focuses on decentering whiteness, power, and privilege, and calls for critical pedagogy and an anti-racist praxis. Arguing that anti-bias education principles do not go far enough, she adds:

Table 2.1. Overview of Culturally Relevant Teaching, Anti-Bias Education, and Anti-Racist Education (CRABAR)

Culturally Relevant Teaching *(Teacher-Centric Supports)*

- Teacher believes all students can learn
- Teacher helps students make connections among their community, national, and global identities
- Teacher demonstrates a connectedness with all students (e.g., emotional, physical, social)
- Teacher encourages a "community of learners"
- Teacher views knowledge, teaching, and learning critically
- Teacher seeks excellence as a complex standard that may involve some postulates but takes student diversity and individual differences into account

(Ladson-Billings, 1994, 2014)

Anti-Bias Education (ABE) *(Child-Centric Supports)*

- ABE Goal 1: Each child will demonstrate self-awareness, confidence, family pride, and positive social identities.
- ABE Goal 2: Each child will express comfort and joy with human diversity; accurate language for human differences; and deep, caring human connections.
- ABE Goal 3: Each child will increasingly recognize unfairness, have language to describe unfairness, and understand that unfairness hurts.
- ABE Goal 4: Each child will demonstrate empowerment and the skills to act, with others or alone, against prejudice and/or discriminatory actions.

(Derman-Sparks, 1989; Derman-Sparks et al., 2020)

Anti-Racist Education *(Race- and Equity-Centric Supports)*

- Racial educational equity at the center of learning and interactions
- Highlighting and critiquing how white power and privilege inform ECE practices in the classroom and in the field
- Education as anti-bias, anti-racist, and culturally relevant
- The curriculum, assessment, classroom environment, and interactions are offered through an anti-bias, anti-racist, and culturally relevant lens
- Educational approach that challenges teachers and children's biases, prejudices, and misperceptions
- Children's cultural and social identities and their capacities for resisting racism are nurtured and sustained
- Teachers and programs have policies, procedures, and practices in place to be aware of and address racism, implicit and explicit biases, prejudices, and stereotypical thinking and actions
- Adults actively watch for internalized prejudice and intervene to address these negative self-perceptions (i.e., when children believe the negative things being said about their race and apply these to themselves)

(Iruka et al., 2020)

Table 2.2. The CRABAR Framework

CRABAR Framework		
Culturally Relevant Teaching	Anti-Bias Education	Anti-Racist Education
Centers the teacher and educational experiences as related to culturally grounded beliefs and instruction. Provides the what and how of instruction and interaction.	Centers the goals and experiences of the child as related to anti-bias education, teaching, and learning. Requires teachers to intentionally implement culturally relevant educational experiences for children Requires teachers to constantly reflect on their own biases and -isms. Teaches children about, or provides a curriculum centered on, *equity, justice, and fairness.*	Centers racial educational equity in the work of educational professionals and experiences for children. Provides a very specific lens and positionality around the role and impact of racism, oppression, and white privilege in early childhood. Focuses on decentering whiteness, power, and privilege.

While I acknowledge teaching children to respect and appreciate human diversity as a commendable goal, the anti-bias curriculum instead poses a danger reminiscent of that associated with "tolerance" rhetoric, which fails to disrupt the meanings attached to racialized "others" and whites. To advance a critical consciousness in the early years, I propose that best practices facilitate critiques of the relationship between white power, privilege, and the construction of the meanings associated with whiteness and anti-blackness discourse. (Escayg, 2019, p. 7)

An anti-racist educational approach encompasses the intentional acts of early childhood professionals to challenge racism, promote racial equity, and create learning experiences for children that are positive, healthy, and racially equitable.

Review Table 2.2 to see how we emphasize culturally relevant teaching, anti-bias education, and anti-racist education in our CRABAR framework.

CRABAR Framework in Action

Let's now explore how the CRABAR framework can be applied within early childhood classrooms. Ladson-Billings (1994) defined *culturally relevant* [teaching] as "pedagogy that empowers students intellectually, socially, emotionally, and politically by using cultural referents to impart knowledge, skills, and attitudes" (pp. 17–18), and Gay (2000) describes what such a pedagogy looks like in terms of being relevant to children's needs in the classroom. Curenton and Iruka (2013) extended these scholars' knowledge and defined *culturally relevant instruction* as teaching that incorporates the cultural knowledge, experiences, and diverse learning and communication styles of children of color, and linked this concept with *anti-bias instruction*, which focuses on racism, stereotypes, and prejudices that exist within our societal structures that fuel disparities and inequities. *Anti-racist instruction* is an approach that explicitly focuses on creating experiences for Black and brown children that promote a positive racial identity (Escayg, 2019). Anti-racist education also dismantles and eliminates curriculum, policies, and practices that are racist and center whiteness at the exclusion and oppression of Black and brown children.

Culturally relevant and anti-bias instruction includes organizing the learning activity so that the content is culturally relevant and socially significant, such as selecting literature that represents culturally familiar situations, roles, and experiences (Ladson-Billings, 2014) or using culturally familiar discourse practices like call-and-response and oral storytelling (Hale, 2001). Language and literacy instructional interactions are especially important to consider when creating culturally relevant anti-bias instruction because oral language discourse is a particular area of classroom communication that is unique for Black and brown children.

When we consider the anti-racist lens, we examine further and highlight the work of Delpit (2006), who explains that often the ways in which racial and ethnic minorities, especially those from low-income environments, express themselves are contrary to the culture of power that exists within classrooms. The *culture of power* within the education system is based on the norms, traditions, values, and heritage of middle- to upper-income white culture. Delpit further articulates that the culture of power within classrooms is enacted during interactions the teacher has with students and through the material within textbooks and curriculum. Because learning is such a language-laden process, these aspects of power are demonstrated in every aspect of language interaction within the classroom, including the linguistic forms that are deemed acceptable in the classroom (Mainstream American English versus African American Vernacular), communicative strategies (e.g., nonverbal behavior, question-answering routines), and the presentation of oneself when speaking, writing, or listening. Heath (1989) provides one of the best descriptions of the language learning process: "When children learn language, they take in more than forms of grammar: They learn to make sense of the social world in which they live and how to adapt to its dynamic social interactions and role relations" (p. 367).

Let's see the CRABAR Framework in action. Consider the following two classroom scenarios. The first example is from a toddler classroom and the second is from a preschool classroom.

SCENARIO 1

Target Group: Toddlers

Topic/Domain: Creativity

Standard: Connect toddlers' imaginary play to their favorite books to connect real-life experiences with those in books.

Learning Experience: The children in Ms. Jennie's toddler classroom love the *Little Blue Truck* books. They ask her to read them several times a day. She finds an old toy truck at the thrift shop and paints it bright blue. The children fill the truck with farm animals like in the book, saying, "moo," "neigh," and "quack quack" as they add new passengers.

In Scenario 1, the standard explicitly asks to focus on creativity, imaginary play, and to connect to real-life experiences. Take a moment to consider what we have explored so far related to culturally relevant teaching, anti-bias education, and anti-racist education. Ms. Jennie begins with a book that the children enjoy reading—fantastic, but what are the children's cultural and linguistic references that she is drawing upon? Culturally relevant teaching would ask and answer the following questions:

- How can she bring the sights, sounds, and experiences of children's families and communities into the lesson?
- What are the trucks or cars the children are familiar with seeing at home or in the community?
- What animals and sounds are they familiar with and see often?
- How about the languages at home and in the community?
- How could she integrate children's home language throughout this lesson (verbally and in written form)?

When we then examine anti-bias education, we further engage children in a diverse range of experiences that do not promote stereotypes. For example, let's imagine that instead of providing one blue truck, Ms. Jennie is intentional about having a diversity of types and colors of trucks and encourages active play and creative expression based on children's age, gender, and cultural background (not assuming that only boys can play with trucks or be

engaged in active play). She encourages children to express themselves and
their interests in a variety of ways that speaks to the multiple identities and
cultural references they bring with them to the classroom. Lastly, from an anti-
racist approach, as children are engaging in active, creative play, Ms. Jennie
would then observe which children are truly interested in the book and topic
because she acknowledges that race or privilege can easily manifest in basic
classroom practices and activities. She therefore critically reflects on whether
children's interest and engagement is based on their race and gender and how
she is engaging Black and brown children equally in scaffolding, conversations,
and supports in this creative expression. As you consider this scenario, what
are ways in which Ms. Jennie could create opportunities to further support
children's positive racial identity in this activity with young children?

Now, let's explore a preschool classroom in Scenario 2.

Scenario 2

Target Group: Preschool: 3- and 4-year-olds

Topic/Domain: Cognitive Development (Science)

Standard: Students will use senses to observe and experience objects and
environments.

Learning Experience: Mr. John has set up three sensory tables for students
to explore during small group today. Table one is the tasting table; he has
asked Marco's grandmother to bake the oatmeal cookies Marco talks about
often during snack time. At table two there is an assortment of items children
have brought from home that begin with the letter A (acorn, avocado, [toy]
ambulance, apple). Table three is the listening area where children can click
on the classroom iPad, listen, and dance to different songs based on a play-
list of favorite songs that Mr. John collected from the children's families.

Let's consider the culturally relevant, anti-bias, and anti-racist aspects of
this learning experience. Can you identify which components of this lesson were culturally relevant? If you identified how Mr. John intentionally
connected the learning experiences to children's homes and experiences by
integrating Marco's grandmother's cookies, the items children brought from
home, and favorite family tunes, then you are right on target! Because these
experiences are culturally meaningful and provide a frame of reference for
children, their connection to and extension of the learning activities are
maximized. Additionally, we can imagine that Mr. John prompts students
to share about the items that have cultural relevance to them and use their
expressive language to describe and experience these items at each table. As
with culturally relevant education, children become naturally curious about

cultural connections that are similar and different from their frame of references and cultural reality. We therefore can image the following scenario that may take place at the first table:

Mr. John: Hello, friends. Check out these delicious cookies that Marco's grandmother made. Marco, what do you call your grandmother?
Marco: Um, Nana.
Mr. John: Why do you like your Nana's cookies so much?
Marco: They are good and I can eat 100!
Mr. John: Well alright then, kiddos, let's taste these yummy cookies! What do you think?
Zoe: I think they are so yummy too; can I have another one?
Mr. John: Let's try just one so others can enjoy them as well. What do you notice about the cookies? What do they look like to you?
Jerome: They are all different shapes, round, triangle.
Marco: My Nana just did that for our class. She don't make them like that.
Susie: Hey, it matches your skin. [Susie places her cookie onto Jerome's arm.]
Jerome: Get that off me, I'm not no brown boo boo monster!

Let's pause here. In this interaction there are two opportunities for Mr. John to proceed in engaging children in anti-bias education and anti-racism. Racial prejudice in young children leads to distortion of their judgment and perceptions of reality, and is firmly rooted in early socialization based on their racial status and experiences (Derman-Sparks et al., 2020). The early childhood classroom plays a critical role in how children begin to make sense of racial dynamics of self and others. In this example, Jerome, a brown-skinned African American, has seemingly associated brown with being negative or scary. Mr. John has the opportunity to explicitly address the socially negative message that Jerome has about his racialized identity. The anti-bias approach is to first question Jerome to better understand his comment. See continued dialogue below:

Mr. John: Jerome, why do you say you are not a brown boo-boo monster?
Jerome: She put that brown cookie on me, but I'm beige and awesome like my dad.

Based on Jerome's response, it is clear what we assumed in that Jerome has associated brown as being negative. Therefore, the next step in anti-bias education is for Mr. John to use this conversation as a teachable moment for Jerome and all children about skin color and the attributes we place on them:

Mr. John: Let's see here [Mr. John looks at his own skin]. So, my skin is more like a graham cracker, and I match my mother. She is so awesome, kind, and smart, nothing like a monster. The cupcakes we had for Kim's birthday yesterday were dark brown and chocolate, they were not scary like a monster, either.

The other kids begin to chime in about all the brown things that they like. Jerome looks on with no comment.

The anti-racist layer is for Mr. John to reflect further on this classroom experience and design more opportunities in his classroom that explicitly promote positive racial identity of children. He would also do an inventory of classroom books and images to ensure that there are pictures and materials representing various shades of brown. Mr. John also notices that many of the characters in the kids' favorite stories that are heroes are of lighter skin tones, and the villains are of darker skin tones. He collects all the books and uses them in a lesson he has designed that prompts children to discuss openly the characteristics of the villain vs. the hero/shero and why this is unfair and not accurate.

The accurate depiction and discussion around the villainization of Black and brown people through story books, cartoons, and pictures is where **anti-racist education** takes anti-bias education to another level. In other words, to be anti-bias is to discuss how unjust and unfair it is to have negative and stereotypical images of Black and brown people; anti-racism examines how inaccurate this description is and provides a counternarrative. Mr. John also is intentional in his efforts to move forward in creating learning experiences for children that explicitly teach them about their cultural history and affirm their shared physical characteristics. These are all strategies associated with positive racial identity development in children (Allen et al., 2021; Escayg, 2019; Hughes et al., 2015). So, for example, instead of the morning circle time that uses Eurocentric nursery rhymes and is often teacher-led, children sing and lead songs that affirm skin tones, are in their native language, and affirm racial pride. The following is an example of a chant that affirms Black racial pride that can be used during circle time or transition:

We are Black
We are unique
We love the way we look,
and we love the way we speak
We created things big and small
So . . . we stand tall!
We are lawyers, inventors,
and teachers from far and wide
We are Black

No one can steal our joy;
no one can steal our pride!

(Escayg, 2022)

The following songs could be used to affirm the multiple languages children bring with them to the classroom while also introducing them to other languages and cultures. Uno, Dos y Tres (https://www.whistlefritz .com/uno-dos-y-tres/) and Two Tigers 两只老虎 (https://www.youtube.com /watch?v=a_SNpbRq86c) provide opportunities to infuse number sense and cardinal counting in Spanish and in Mandarin. Che Che Kule allows children to use bodies and movement for creative expression and learning while also teaching an African language. In the next chapter, we provide more concrete examples of these practices and learning experiences across early childhood content domains.

CRABAR Framework for Families

So far, we have explored the CRABAR framework within the context of teaching, learning, and educational systems. It is important to also examine CRABAR for families. As a way to put CRABAR into action when engaging families of REM learners, Curenton, Iruka, and Eke (2014) suggest using their Culturally Responsive Anti-bias Family Engagement 4Es approach (*Exploration, Expectation, Education,* and *Empowerment*), called CRAF-E4 (Iruka, 2022a).

Exploration. To partner with families, ECE professionals must be open to asking families about their hopes, dreams, and goals for themselves and children. Most ECE organizations and entities do a family needs assessment or interest surveys; however, programs should find out what families know, do, and how best to support their family and children. ECE professionals should always ask families what they are doing to meet their children's needs and build off familial practices based on a family's knowledge, beliefs, traditions, and norms. A true partnership between families and ECE professional can only happen through respect and trust. This partnership is critical for racially and ethnically minoritized families whose culture, experiences, and practices are often ignored or not valued.

Self-inquiry Questions:

- How can you make sure that your program is ensuring equitable experiences for all families?
- That is, how do you make sure that your program is partnering with families based on what families know, do, and bring?

- Do you ask every family to tell you about themselves each month?
- What questions do you ask them to learn more about them?
- Do you ask families what parts of the programs or services are working best for them?
- Whose voices are not heard often about programs and services, and how can you make sure they are heard more often?

Expectation. Studies show that parent and educator high expectations are important for children's learning competence and academic success. When professionals hold families to high expectations, families will meet and surpass those expectations. ECE professionals' expectations must be connected to families' goals for their children and themselves. The ECE professionals and families need to work together to figure out how families can meet the goals in the way that considers families' knowledge and skills, as well as the time, resources, and supports they have. For example, if parents have a goal for their child to enjoy reading, then ECE professionals and parents can come up with a plan that fits how comfortable parents are with reading, considers other family members, caregivers, and family routines that can support reading, and finds books that interest the child. The ECE professional and family should routinely check in to see if the plan worked and how to adjust it.

Self-inquiry questions: As an ECE professional, what do you expect of families in supporting their child's health and safety and emotional, behavioral, social, cognitive, and academic competence skills? Do you see parents as their child's first teacher? If not, why? What past experience or bias may influence how you approach family engagement? Are the expectations of families based on your values rather than families' values (e.g., parents must read a book before bedtime, all family members eat at the table at the same time)? How are you making sure that your expectations are aligned with families' goals and reflect all of the knowledge, skills, and resources, including available time, that families have?

Education. While it is important to ask families about their goals and dreams, the partnership between families and ECE professionals is a two-way street. Information concerning children's school experience, progress and engagement should always be shared with families, especially information on how the school and teacher are supporting children's positive development and learning. Research shows that the more parents know, the more they are likely to do. For example, parents who know how to keep their children safe and healthy, such as by getting immunizations, using car seats/seat belts, and keeping poisonous chemicals away, are likely to follow this advice (Epstein, 2019). Also, the more information parents have about what can support their children's development and learning, such as brain development and early intervention services, the more they are likely to use this information (Epstein, 2019). Thus, ECE professionals are critical in sharing important information with families by translating these research findings in a way that families can use to support their own practices and their children's development and learning. For example, ECE professionals can provide guidance on what quality education involves and how they can find high quality programs and services that meet their and their children's needs. Likewise, ECE providers can tell families about the proven benefits of bilingualism and the important role that using and building children's home language development can have on academic success.

Self-inquiry Questions: Who do you share the latest research information with? Do you share with all families or some families? If you choose which families you share information with, is there a reason for this? Are there unstated "rules" that determine who gets to access certain resources and supports (e.g., those who have a job vs. unemployed, two-parent vs. one-parent household)? How does the information shared build families' networks, knowledge, and resources to meet their families' goals and enhance children's development and learning?

Empowerment. The majority of family engagement programs and services are focused on empowerment, which helps parents feel confident and strong in advocating for themselves, their child, and the community. It is critical to ensure that all families, regardless of their race, ethnicity, language, social class, or any other demographic marker, feel connected to the ECE community. Each family must feel valued and unique and contribute to the quality of the ECE environment regardless of who they are and what they bring. ECE professionals, programs, and organizations must create an environment of belonging, making sure that families have the knowledge, resources, and tools—to be empowered—to do their best and address any problems in their way.

Self-inquiry Questions: How do you know you have created an environment where all families, including children of diverse racial, ethnic, language, disability, and socioeconomic status backgrounds are made to feel like they belong? How do you make sure that you and your program and organizations are welcoming and make every family feel like they are important, are valued, and belong?

The CRAF-E4 helps teachers learn how to:

- Appreciate the strengths and capabilities found among diverse families
- Recognize how societal oppression and injustices create family hardship and stress

- Empower families and children to have equal participation in education decision-making

CRAF-E4 not only provides a great framework for educators and schools, but also provides a basis for understanding the role of other family members and their contribution to the educational excellence of Black students. Black families have a unique cultural experience shaped by their involvement in American society, but also by a rich African heritage. Black families experience stressors that are confounded with poverty and inequalities in the social determinants of health, such as unemployment, lower levels of education attainment, inadequate access to health care, and psychological stressors compounded by racism. Teachers who are working with a family that includes REM learners should be aware of the life circumstances of the families they are working with, especially families living and raising a child in poverty, and their learning and communication styles. A relationship with a family that includes a REM learner must begin with empathy, honesty, and action.

- Empathy is needed to alleviate the ongoing bias, prejudice, discrimination, marginalization, and racism families and their children face.
- Honesty is needed to validate the impact of all of this on Black and brown families and their children.
- Empathy and honesty must be a springboard for action. Everything a program does must confirm to families that it is anti-bias, anti-racist, culturally relevant, culturally sustaining, and equitable.

These principles—empathy, honesty, and action—are seen across the foundational position and policy statements of the National Association for the Education of Young Children (NAEYC, 2019), which have been embraced by early childhood educators.

NOW WHAT?

Implementing educational equity requires a critical lens and approach to learning that addresses not only the need to be culturally responsive to young children and families, but also the need to teach children to be fair and just. It is also critical to explicitly and intentionally address instances of racism that permeate early childhood education and policies that contribute to systemic racial inequities. "Best practices" and approved curriculums may reflect these unfairnesses; in many instances, "best practices" are based on a white-centric lens that does not account for diverse customs and ideas about child development. Approval of curricula is usually done through a white-governed process that does not fully and authentically consider CRABAR theoretical and pedagogical approaches.

Furthermore, the ways in which we measure quality of programs and teachers are grounded in a Eurocentric perspective. For example, most program and school curriculum and assessments are presented monolingually (standard English) and monoculturally (individualist). Eurocentric expectations become problematic for programs and teachers serving REM learners who represent multiple languages and literacies and a more collectivist cultural affinity. Therefore, we must be intentional and explicit in examining how our policies, programming, and quality measures represent the diversity in knowledge and experiences REM learners and teachers bring with them.

In anti-racism and anti-bias work, we intentionally identify whether a teacher, practice, or policy is biased or racist through ongoing and critical reflection and examination. Let's imagine that we first own and then address beliefs before they develop into practices, policies, and programs that are harmful to Black and brown children.

EDUCATORS' CORNER

Earlier in this chapter we asked you to reflect upon your emotional reactions to the terms *racism* and *bias*. Reflect back on your intitial reactions to hearing the terms racism and bias at the beginning of this chapter. Has your reaction changed? Is there anything else you would add? As you reflect on your own experiences and positionality related to bias and racism in early childhood, consider these three important statements:

STATEMENT 1: Racism and bias exist in our schools and early learning programs. I have seen evidence of racism and bias in my professional setting(s).

STATEMENT 2: Racism and bias have negatively impacted Black and brown children and families.

STATEMENT 3: I can make a positive difference in my work as a culturally relevant, anti-bias, and anti-racist teacher, but I must first engage in critical self-reflection so I can identify the areas in which my social identity/identities may be informing my practice

---

Pause. Reflect. Anti-racism and anti-racist teaching should be implemented in all classrooms, however, due to the deeply entrenched racist structures of the United States and beyond, not all teachers believe in either the value or significance of anti-racist work. We therefore ask you to consider the following: What are your immediate reactions, thoughts, and beliefs concerning the statements above? Are they similar to or different than when you hear the terms racism and bias? It is important that your beliefs about teaching and learning are aligned with these three statements. How would you respond to a fellow educator who makes a comment such as "racism no longer exists"?

If you doubt or actively challenge the idea that racism and bias exist and have impacted Black and brown children, you cannot begin the work of implementing the CRABAR framework. Indeed, instead of being a vehicle of change and justice, you will become an instrument of silence, violence, and exclusion, thereby perpetuating additional harm against children's minds, hearts, and souls. If you believe that bias and/or racism only exist outside of your classroom, school, or early learning program, you are not prepared to be a culturally relevant, anti-bias, anti-racist teacher or leader. If you believe you can make a difference but are unsure what next steps to take, continue forward to Chapter 3, which will provide additional insights on how to embed culturally relevant, anti-bias, and anti-racist educational experiences in your learning environments to advance children's growth, development, and well-being.

As you proceed further in this book, we encourage you to continue to identify your *what*, then your *why*, concerning beliefs and experiences with bias and racism in early childhood. For example, *why* do you want to do this work? *What* motivates you? *What* inspires you? Understanding your *what* and *why* will help prepare you to move forward in addressing the *how* of being culturally relevant, anti-bias, and anti-racist in early childhood. Onward and upward!

CHAPTER 3

Creating CRABAR
Learning Environments

"Hola, Isabella. ¿Como estas?," asks Mr. Pitts. [Isabella is a five-year-old preschool student who recently joined the class and Mr. Pitts wants to ensure she feels as comfortable in the classroom as the other kids.] "I am okay," Isabella responds. "I love looking at this picture on this wall because it reminds me of mi abuelo and I would ride the tractor with him and my other cousins when we visited his farm in Nebraska." Mr. Pitts smiles at Isabella and says, "Wonderful to know you love that picture on the wall, let's see if there are other memories you can tell me about when you look at the other pictures on the wall." Mr. Pitts tries to find moments throughout the school year to do a walk around the classroom with each student to look at and talk about the pictures on the walls. He wants each student to see a happy story of themselves in at least one piece of the wall art.

What does this scenario make you think of? What images and emotions does it call to mind? We ask you to consider such narrative because when prompted to reflect on their teaching experiences, most educators—without the slightest hint of reservation—would unequivocally state that they would like their students to experience a sense of safety, joy, and belonging in their classrooms. Learning materials, including texts, as suggested in the opening narrative, point to one pedagogical strategy; yet, to fully embed anti-racist practices, one must consider the interrelated features of the classroom environment. Such is the purpose of this chapter. As you read this chapter, we encourage you to pause, question, critique, and engage in the process of self-discovery—one which is one often fraught with tensions, discomfort, and uncertainties, we readily admit; but it is also helpful to consider that self-reflection directed toward transformation also births new awareness of ourselves and our practices.

Among contributions to peer-reviewed research on racial socialization, the most significant work typically comes from bold scholarship that open-ly challenges racist narratives of racially marginalized or disenfranchised parents while highlighting the specific ways in which the home environment contributes to children's racial consciousness. As young children return to both childcare and classroom contexts in this new pandemic world, families have begun to scrutinize how often their young children encounter welcoming and responsive teaching practices. For example, what types of classroom environments and pedagogy do racially minoritized children experience? What social and emotional outcomes do these early learning spaces cultivate about children's sense of self, including how they value and understand their cultural identities? In light of these pertinent concerns, this chapter examines anti-racist teaching practices and provides suggestions for designing and implementing classroom environments that support anti-racist education goals of systemic change, justice, resistance, and positive racial identity.

SPACES FOR BELONGING: MODEL LEARNING ENVIRONMENTS

What do children know about race? How do they acquire and make use of such knowledge in their everyday lives? Research addressing the intersections of race and parenting among Black families, for example, has shown that Black parents/caregivers routinely engage in discussions about race, racism, and racial identity with their children. Indeed, Peters's (1985) definition of such practices, termed "racial socialization" in the literature, still rings true today: "The responsibility of raising physically and emotionally healthy children who are Black in a society in which Black has negative connotations" (p. 161). Hughes et al.'s (2006) conceptual framework has served as the pre-eminent resource for identifying common parenting strategies, including assisting children with navigating and coping with racism (*preparation for bias*), building racial pride (*cultural socialization*), avoiding discussions about race (*silence on race*), and emphasizing equality among different racial groups (*egalitarianism*). Hughes's framework continues to guide research aimed at exploring how parents equip children with necessary knowledge about race and racism. The present chapter builds on seminal contributions to anti-racist literature—especially those critical to the early childhood education (ECE) field—to better articulate practical strategies for creating and implementing an anti-racist classroom environment, one which supports positive parent–teacher interactions, children's social and emotional well-being, and similar to the racial socialization literature, positive racial-ethnic identity development among racially minoritized children.

We first begin with a survey of the current scholarship on anti-racist ECE contexts and follow with an analysis of equity issues in the classroom environment, offering a closer look at the extant literature to build on new lines of inquiry related to social–emotional learning and anti-racism. This chapter also provides a framework for creating anti-racist early years learning environments. An anti-racist ECE practice will explicitly name and challenge racism through pedagogical approaches, content of the curriculum, and family engagement practices. Although anti-bias and anti-racist approaches to ECE share common goals, such as fostering positive social identities, anti-racist early childhood education centers issues of race and racism, identifies, and challenges how racism functions in classroom practices, policy, and the disciplinary knowledge base. By specifically foregrounding race, however, anti-racist early childhood practice aims to disrupt racism through institutional and pedagogical reforms (Escayg, 2019, 2020a).

PAUSE AND CONSIDER

What does your current teaching environment look like? What was the process of selecting materials for each learning center? Was the rationale for selecting these materials equitable? Does this space allow children to see themselves positively represented and if so, how? What messages does it convey?

The aim of such a procedural approach to analyzing systemic racism is to address gaps in access to anti-racist ECE curricula and to scaffold anti-racist early years practices via concrete frameworks. For instance, one of the renowned scholars of anti-racist education in the Canadian context, George J. Sefa Dei, whose integrative teaching and research contributions to racialized schooling activities in "theory and practice" (1996) advocates for systemic change by calling out the various manifestations of racism in schooling contexts (for example, the lack of an inclusive anti-racist curriculum and the pathologizing of racially minoritized families and youth) and outlining anti-racist solutions at interpersonal, cultural, and institutional levels. Given the scope of this chapter, we will also explore processes of assessment (by deconstructing them) and the design of anti-racist early years environments (a creative form of reconstruction). To encourage reader reflection throughout, chapter subheadings prompt deeper considerations of anti-racist pedagogy.

THE CLASSROOM ENVIRONMENT: A REVIEW

Many educational studies suggest that the classroom environment constitutes one of the focal components in supporting positive early-years outcomes within the context of schooling. An effective environment typically involves delineating spaces to allow for inclusive learning material and classroom design. This process is usually conceptualized as an important "structural" aspect of the classroom environment (Manning et al., 2019), and prioritized in the name of quality relationships between students and teachers (Dörnyei

& Muir, 2019; Dynia et al., 2018; Guo et al., 2012). Indeed, such concepts reflect multidimensional applications of the classroom environment, which researchers have linked to student engagement and achievement (Aydoğan et al., 2015; Reyes et al., 2012); language and literacy skills (Guo et al., 2015); and social-emotional development (Rucinski et al., 2018).

For example, Aydoğan et al. (2015) found that the "instructional support and the emotional tone of the classroom/teacher were associated with classroom levels of children's engagement in learning in kindergarten" (p. 613). Earlier findings culled from studies conducted with the participation of preschool-aged children in a play-based setting (Morrow; 1990; Morrow & Rand, 1991) also revealed that teacher guidance and literacy materials influence how children use play as a vehicle to engage in and express nascent literacy skills. Interrogating the urgent need for encouraging and strengthening responsive teacher–student relationships, Rucinski et al. (2018) posit that the overall emotional climate of the classroom alone does not predict positive child outcomes, arguing instead that *individual teacher–student relationships* foster optimal social–emotional functioning and academic success.

Despite the growing body of evidence indicating how the classroom environment supports children's development in various domains, what remains a perceptible gap (although the concept of "psychological environment" bears a degree of practical relevance) is the lack of empirical data on the effect of teaching and learning contexts on children's racial identity development in general, and Black children's identity in particular. To date, scholars have yet to fully examine how Afrocentric learning environments steeped in rich cultural and ancestral knowledge and history influence the ways that Black children ascribe value and meaning to their identities, while also developing an awareness of racial group membership and their place in overarching sociopolitical narratives of resistance and racial solidarity. In the interest of addressing the ongoing question of how to fill pedagogical gaps in anti-racist early childhood education, we explore how anti-racist classroom environments bring to light the possibilities and positive effects of racially affirming curricular material and classroom spaces. Accordingly, we offer the following brief autoethnographic anecdote.

REFLECTION ON AFROCENTRIC CLASSROOM ENVIRONMENTS

Kerry-Ann Escayg: Recently, I paid a visit to an African-centered school as part of preliminary research for a study on the relationship between African-centered play-based learning and children's racial identity. When I entered the classroom, the children's enthusiasm and joy were palpable. They relayed a clear message: "We are safe, and we are happy here." And how was that sense of security central to learning, I wondered?

At the back of the classroom, a mirror caught my eye, and hanging next to it was a series of empowering affirmations. In the library center, I found the rightfully popular text, *Hair Love* (Cherry & Harrison, 2019). What captured my attention next, however, was a self-portrait by a young girl. At the bottom of the drawing—a beautiful brown face with a wide, beaming grin—was a hand-lettered statement: "It is okay to have short hair." I approached the child responsible for making the picture, opening with, "You drew this?" Offering an equally enthusiastic smile, one which communicated an emotion she may not have articulated yet, but that was nonetheless unmistakable to onlookers, she responded, "Yes, I did!" That illuminating smile hinted at the subtext accompanying her vocal affirmation: She was proud, and she was challenging conventional expectations.

Equitable settings promote positive self-concepts and challenge dominant social and ideological narratives around race, class, gender, and language. Ideally, anti-racist early years classroom environments provide children with a range of opportunities to celebrate, respect, and honor diverse social identities (including their own). By contrast, what passes for a learning space in educational and early childcare contexts alike, including play-based settings, is a predominantly "race-silenced" environment with pervasive whiteness as the norm (Escayg, 2018), essentially negating racialized and marginalized children's identities and excluding them from curricular materials, classroom design, and teaching and learning activities. Early childhood educators must take responsibility for how young children fare—spiritually, emotionally, and academically—in their learning contexts.

In the absence of anti-racist classroom spaces, young racially and ethnically minoritized children's identity development—the latter considered a significant component of overall social–emotional well-being—may be rendered increasingly susceptible to prevailing racial discourses that seek to maintain whiteness as the preferred or ideal identity by default. Also, in such prejudicial classroom spaces, a lack of explicit and concrete examples of anti-racist imagery, materials, and classroom discussions contributes to white children further internalizing and reproducing the racialized power dynamics characteristic of American society (which, in turn, often translates into psychological harm to Black and racially minoritized children).

PREPARE TO DEVELOP ANTI-RACIST
CLASSROOM ENVIRONMENTS

How do teachers hold space for anti-racist education in the early years? Clearly, addressing anti-racist praxis in the early years and beyond not only requires that we center teachers' critical self-reflection processes, but also calls for a recognition of how systems and structures may restrict educators' attempts at disrupting racialized educational norms. It is also imperative for us to remind readers that for some educators, the classroom environment outwardly mirrors their internal beliefs, worldviews, and racial attitudes. In other words, what matters most to an educator tends to manifest externally (in the materials that they choose, such as readings or toys for play centers, for instance). For anti-racist educators, despite a deep-seated desire to create empowering, racially affirming environments, prohibitive funding and a corresponding lack of space serve as the defining factors.

As the richness and transformative power of an anti-racist curriculum for students can only be realized via an anti-racist classroom environment (which is created by the instructor), we turn our focus toward self-reflection. We find these exercises helpful in both personal and professional journeys toward anti-racist practice. Indeed, we acknowledge that inward-focused reflections that help educators identify their own preconceptions also help to envision early years classrooms as anti-racist learning environments.

EXAMINING SELF AND STRUCTURES

Prepare to establish anti-racist classroom environments by doing the following:

1. Reflect on the goal of the anti-racist classroom environment
2. Convey connections between curriculum, lesson planning, and environment
3. Stage a learning site (as key to children's social-emotional development)
4. Adhere to an anti-racist redesign or restoration process

We expand on this four-dimensional approach and offer practical examples to guide educators through the processes of assessing, designing, evaluating, and improving their classroom environments.

Above all, anti-racism will inform the core features of any equitable teaching practice, thereby improving children's learning experiences.

1. Reflect on the Goal of the Anti-Racist Classroom Environment

Much of the anti-racist educational literature supports teachers' self-reflection. Such a process enables educators to identify the connections between any underlying racial biases and their teaching practices. We further argue that any process of self-introspection should involve an *assessment of how pedagogical belief systems may inform classroom design*. More pointedly, with few exceptions, (e.g., Lara-Cinisomo et al., 2009), there remains limited scholarly discussion detailing how educators conceptualize the classroom environment as an integral dimension of the teaching and learning process. This gap exists despite available findings attesting to the potentially significant role played by the classroom environment in promoting high-quality learning experiences. Classroom environments are important for children's learning and development, *and* racist classroom environments will impact children's learning, including their racial identity.

In an insightful qualitative study on childhood educators' beliefs about preschoolers' classroom experiences, Lara-Cinisomo et al. (2009) discover how some educators specify which dimensions of the classroom environment are integral to promoting kindergarten readiness, including "safety, age appropriateness, teacher resourcefulness, clear rules and consequences, and predictability" targets (p. 4). Perhaps these findings are attributable in part to the fact that in the ECE field, measuring tools such as the Early Childhood Environment Rating Scale (ECERS) (Harms et al., 1998) and the Classroom Assessment Scoring System (CLASS) (Hamre & Pianta, 2007) have been so widely used in empirical investigations that educators have developed a modicum of familiarity with these measures in their initial preservice training. Moreover, the different environmental dimensions that many educators identify, including procedures and design, helpfully dovetail with the theoretical subscales of the ECERS (revised edition), including (1) space and furnishings; (2) personal care and routines; (3) language and reasoning; (4) activities; (5) student interactions; (6) program structure; and (7) parental/staff influences. One of the subscales on the CLASS scoring system focuses on classroom organization.

While these are excellent contributions to the field of pedagogical approaches, the manner in which such rating systems typically omit children's racial and cultural identities is both worthy of critique and salient to the present discussion. More specifically, such rating scales, when examined carefully, indicate how positionality, power, and privilege shape and influence the processes of knowledge production generally and in the development of classroom environmental measures in particular.

We also observe a lack of educators' voices in defining what constitutes a positive and supportive classroom environment. We appeal for more holistic, qualitative processes to ensure educators can examine their underlying beliefs about *classroom authority* (i.e., the identities that they embody), their methods of *classroom design* (including benchmarks and evaluations), and the *goals* that they hope to achieve professionally (and with individual students). For instance, early childhood educators might consider the following questions:

- What is the function of the classroom environment?
- What is the relationship between the classroom space and the concept of belonging?

- What is the quality of classroom interaction—both verbal and non-verbal—for students?
- What is the classroom messaging to students about themselves and their social worlds?
- Does my classroom environment promote global/civic citizenship and if so, how?
- Do students engage in class discussions on social justice issues (local, national, global)?

Regarding the spatial dimensions of learning sites and furnishings, from an anti-racist perspective, educators should, at minimum, consider how traditional linear seating arrangements may be at odds with African and Indigenous cultural values. These forms of classroom arrangement reveal clearly the long-standing legacies of white American culture, for example, individualism and the myth of meritocracy, influencing schooling processes and classroom design. In contrast, traditional emphases on collectivism and group well-being are cultural practices of the African Diaspora, which educators often fail to recognize and implement in their classrooms. By contrast, and in keeping with an anti-racist and African-centered approach, educators can use circle/group seating arrangements to promote a more "community" oriented environment. This holds the potential to promote group-centered learning, which, according to Brandt (1986), is the "teaching style or pedagogic device" that best supports the realization of anti-racist teaching (p. 145). Additionally, safety should be reconceptualized from a vantage point that recognizes the ongoing psychological pain and trauma that Black, Indigenous, and REM children encounter at school and in early years contexts. While we are not dismissing the importance of physical safety, we propose that children's mental, emotional, and spiritual well-being are equally important aspects to consider, especially when evaluating the effectiveness of early childhood learning environments. In other words, how does your classroom environment make a child feel? Does it foster joy, a sense of discovery, wonder, and racial and cultural connections? And, for Black children, does your classroom environment help children see themselves as part of a racial group, and in so doing, cultivate racial pride, and their own form of resistance and group solidarity? As you ponder on these questions, and the role of facilitating joyful learning experiences for Black children, consider the following interview data from Escayg's (2020b) study with African American children. The child participant had indicated that her teacher had introduced the class to the contributions of African Americans. As a follow-up question, the researcher asked the child: "And when you are learning about these, how does it make you feel?" To which the child responded:

"It makes me feel proud that I am Black. It makes me feel like yay mostly not yay, it's like yippee!"(Blacklivesmatter)

Note: In keeping with the best practices associated with conducting research with children, along with an anti-racist research design, children were given the opportunity to choose their own pseudonym.

2. Convey Connections Among Curriculum, Lesson Planning, and Environment

Consistency is key to the successful implementation of even the soundest of pedagogical practices. Similarly, cultivating and sustaining an equitable classroom environment contributes to lasting anti-racist child outcomes. More plainly, in an anti-racist learning environment, whatever students see reproduced externally, through images on the wall, in materials, via furnishings and spatial arrangements, or through teacher–student interactions, is also incorporated into formal and informal curricula (namely, in daily routines such as circle time, end-of-day procedures, lesson plans, and transitions). However, anti-racist teaching in the early years needs to be both visible and effective. It is obligatory for teachers to initially assess the quality of the curriculum materials currently in use (Husband & Escayg, 2022).

Since its groundbreaking emergence at conferences, summits, and symposiums in the early 1990s, reconceptualist scholarship in education remains at the forefront of challenges to the overwhelming influence of developmental psychology, developmentally appropriate practice, and the overall Eurocentric underpinnings of early childhood curricula (Kinkead-Clark & Escayg, 2021). As a result of such pioneering action, significant administrative progress has been made in recent years, including the revisions to the National Association for the Education of Young Children's position statement, which now includes guidelines consistent with the goals of the anti-bias curriculum in that it advocates for empowering children to value their social identities while ensuring that they are well-equipped to "counter the biases in society" (NAEYC, 2020, p. 22). However, the need for a national task force on anti-racist and anti-bias curricula remains significant as researchers continue to demonstrate how often young Black children confront curricular violence in early childhood spaces (Boutte & Bryan, 2019).

To address such inequities, Husband and Escayg (2022) recommend an anti-racist curriculum model for early childhood, with chief instructive elements tapping into the enriching potential of racial healing and resistance. Charting the principal ideas of this model effectively reveals the interconnected instructional threads associated with teaching and learning. The curriculum and the classroom environment work in tandem to promote a welcoming, inclusive, and anti-racist experience for young racially minoritized children. For an in-depth critical analysis, see the concluding section on anti-racist redesign processes. Additionally, Table 3.1 offers a few ideas for your classroom practice.

3. Consider Children's Social-Emotional Development

Recognizing the salience of the early years in relation to children's physical, social-emotional, language, and cognitive domains of development, researchers have sought to examine the processes and contexts that best support children in acquiring age-related developmental competencies. For instance, although the home environment is often viewed as the most influential regarding verbal and fine motor skills; recent work examines how the intersection of home and school contexts influences young children's social–emotional development (Bobbitt & Gershoff, 2016). Addressing a broad social construct in their review of the literature, Halle and Darling-Churchill (2016) identify common behavioral subdomains typically associated with social–emotional development, including emotional competence, social competence, and self-regulation.

Social competence generally includes skills related to pro-social behavior, such as perspective-taking, empathy, and cooperation, whereas *emotional* competence involves recognizing one's emotions, regulating those feelings, and recognizing the sentiments of others. Recently, however, scholars have reconceptualized social–emotional learning by repositioning children's racial identity and other contextual factors—including racism—at the forefront of student development, learning, and school success (Jagers et al., 2019; Mayes et al., 2022). Since such an applied approach to social–emotional learning inevitably deconstructs core concepts or "transforms paradigms" (Jagers et al., 2019), this chapter explains how educators can design an anti-racist environment conducive to a positive public and private regard for their students' social identities while also promoting the social justice or resistance-oriented consciousness germane to advancing future antiracist teaching both individually and collectively.

In practice, transformative social–emotional learning dovetails with anti-racist evaluative features and attendant teaching methods. Based on emancipatory theoretical models, the aim is to provide equitable learning opportunities for young children and youth by underscoring:

- historical and current manifestations of racialized inequities
- the prevalence of these inequities in institutional contexts such as schools and early years settings and systems

Table 3.1. Model for Nurturing Positive Social Identities

Curriculum Content Area	Play Centers (Affirming Identities)	Play Materials	Centering Black Diaspora Cultural Artforms considerations
Preschool (play-based curriculum)	Play centers that reflect children's racial identities (K.-A. Escayg, personal communication, April 21, 2021), including hairdressing or styling centers. See *Hair Love* (Cherry & Harrison, 2019) or *Don't touch my hair!* (Miller, 2019) for guiding precepts. Storytelling centers (Escayg, 2022). Literacy/creative expression centers that incorporate examples of resistance to racial injustices (children can either write or draw how they can stand up to racism).	Diverse play materials, including puzzles (for representative resources, go to https://puzzlehuddle.com). Crayons, markers, dolls, and food items. Books that represent children of diverse racial backgrounds. Picture books that represent Black families' kinship networks. Posters on the wall that reflect children's racial and cultural identities. Wall posters that include specific anti-racist terms along with concrete representations (K.-A. Escayg, personal communication, October 15, 2021).	Music, dance, and technology: For example, considering using music and technology to support phonics instructions (see Gracie's corner: https://www.youtube.com/watch?v=ptk68qC1wol&t=88s). For dance and movement, "Bino and Fino" offers an excellent resource: https://www.youtube.com/watch?v=EmAwTeFVIKA

- the ways in which a series of traditional Social and Emotional
  Learning (SEL) competencies—self-awareness, self-management,
  social awareness, responsible decision-making, and relationship
  skills—can be reframed to center identity, resistance, agency,
  belonging, and engagement in the teaching and learning process
  (Jagers et al., 2019).

The revised SEL competencies are fundamentally oriented toward societal
and educational change while also optimizing children's social–emotional
development. Williams and Jagers (2022) note that a transformative approach to SEL advises that individuals "go beyond being prosocial to their
neighbor but participate in actions that attempt to resist, disrupt, and dismantle the inequities perpetuated by a dominant culture that keeps their
neighbor in an oppressed, marginalized position" (p. 193).

As with curriculum design, the design of a classroom environment
aligned with anti-racist principles offer opportunities for children to
thrive and flourish in each area of the transformative SEL competencies.
Nonetheless, the following passage—italicized here for emphasis—illustrates
how classroom materials, such as picture books, often fail to develop and
nurture social constructs such as agency, belonging, engagement, and racial
identity.

> I am sad, and the sadness makes me not want to play or work with anyone; look,
> look at our classroom; nothing here looks like me! All those books in our library
> and the only pictures of kids like me are bad, are Black Knights! (Earick, 2010,
> p. 135)

Scholarship on Black identity development also yields guiding principles for interpreting the varied conceptual and empirical literature on
children's racial awareness and attitudes. Because much early work has
been conceptualized by psychologists who often theorize identity along a
developmental continuum (although few theoretical applications address
contextual factors), research on racial identity development is typically
conducted with the participation of adults and adolescents. Indeed, a review of the literature shows that even among the more popular measures
in assessing racial identity among adults, the Multidimensional Inventory
of Black Identity (MIBI) (Sellers et al., 1998) stands out for incorporating
the subscales of racial regard (public and private), and racial ideology.

Additionally, Scottham et al. (2008) tender an adolescent-friendly version of the MIBI index, the Multidimensional Inventory of Black Identity-
teen (MIBI-t). By way of differentiation from the original MIBI, the MIBI-t
scale includes only 21 items to make the scale easier to administer and simplify

the abstract concepts found on the adult continuum (ideology, for one) so it is developmentally appropriate and thus may yield more profound insights into our younger students' perceptions of racial dynamics.

Anti-racist early years scholars maintain that self-awareness also encompasses children's racial identity. Nevertheless, only recently have scholars begun to conduct systematic investigations into how social-emotional constructs—reconceptualized to address issues of race, identity, power, and privilege—can support racial identity development among adolescents (e.g., Rivas-Drake et al., 2020; Sun et al., 2022).

Despite the educational and social-emotional benefits of the pedagogical approaches, the effects of an anti-racist social–emotional curriculum on young Black children's racial self-identification and attitudes remain a comparatively unexamined aspect of scholarly inquiry. To address these ample gaps from an anti-racist pedagogical stance, we propose to draw upon the organizational literature pertaining to classroom design while also applying the transformative SEL competencies as they relate to identity and agency (see Table 3.2).

Table 3.2. Classroom Essentials

Transformative SEL Competencies	Classroom Environment Directives
Identity development for ethnically and racially minoritized children	(1) Print photos of children and their families to hang in the classroom (and/or outside the classroom). (2) Plan teacher-led discussions on skin color and hair texture using Persona Dolls (Smith, 2017). (3) Model or provide empowerment both visually and orally for Black identities. (4) Incorporate the contributions of Black people into the curriculum (for example, during morning message/circle time) (5) Study images and texts depicting Black joy and success.
Agency conceptualized as resistance to racism, informed by African American children's perceptions of whiteness (Escayg, 2020b)	(1) Create play areas that stimulate discussions on social issues, such as a justice center (Escayg, 2021). (2) Engage children in problem-solving (What can you/ we do to stop racism?). (3) Introduce children to anti-racist activists in person and digitally (welcoming community anti-racist leaders to share their stories). (4) Teach from exemplary models of children's literature to discuss concepts such as power and privilege.

4. Design Anti-Racist Classroom Environments

Specific structural arrangements of the classroom environment are integral to any anti-racist teaching practice. Therefore, we advise that educators—via their individual dispositions, knowledge, and behaviors—accept responsibility for creating anti-racist learning environments situated within humanized spaces proclaiming Black and racially minoritized children's humanity. In these spaces, educators have open and honest conversations about race and racism, respond to students' comments and curiosities about physical differences, for example, such as skin color and hair texture, and engage families in authentic, family-centered relationships, recognizing and honoring their cultural strengths and practices. Honoring children's humanity means honoring their racialized experiences—not dismissing these on the account of "color-blindness" or any other belief or practice that denies the significance of race and racism in the United States and, arguably, the global context. Anti-racist classroom aides, caregivers, instructors, and leaders enrich the educational experiences of racially minoritized children as valuable agents of change (in collaboration with administrators and institutional support on a systemic level). Of necessity, such interdisciplinary practices will also coincide with the transformative expression of social–emotional competencies, most notably identity, belonging, and agency. Yet, it should be noted that effective anti-racist instruction requires educators being aware of their own social-emotional skills (see Caven, 2020).

Attending to these critical gaps in the literature, Legette et al. (2022) argue that quality teacher–student interactions, predicated on affirming the humanity of Black youth, are foundational to cultivating their social–emotional competencies. For instance, Warren et al. (2022) examined the ways in which high school teachers' dispositions revealed insights into not only their SEL competencies but also expressions of transformative social-emotional learning. The researchers discovered that teachers' self-awareness—in one example, their racial and gender identities—influenced how they perceived their role as an educator and, as a result, informed the nature and quality of their interactions with students.

Furthermore, educators' sense of identity, belonging, engagement, and agency—all favorably transformative SEL competencies—enrich many teachers' classroom practices: "When asked in our exit interview what he wanted most for the Black boys he teaches, Mr. Julian [a Black educator] remarked, 'I just want them to be free'" (Warren et al., 2022, p. 268). Although such commentary highlights the educator's concern for his students' holistic well-being and aligns conceptually with the dimension of classroom agency (Warren et al., 2022, p. 268), it is important to note how the interrelated aspects of SEL apparently work together to inform a teacher's racial identity—or embodied racialized knowledge—and influence his aspirations for students and their prospective achievements.

Shared racialized experiences intersect within a relational structure that allows for student-centered perspectives based on warm and positive teacher–pupil relationships. However, in cases where the values typified by a given teaching faculty do not reflect those of the student population, how can transformative SEL dimensions be operationalized to inform anti-racist teaching? First, we acknowledge that white educators can and should be anti-racist. Second, using the dimension of identity/self-awareness, for instance, we emphasize the need for an "unveiling" or unmasking of whiteness for educators. This means that educators must recognize that "white" is a racialized identity, one endowed with both privilege and power—and should not be construed as the "standard" or the "norm" (Escayg, 2019; Hazelbaker et al., 2022). Relatedly, as part of this process, it is important that white educators learn about, identify, and critique the varied dimensions of white privilege, and see how they can, from a posture of racial humility, use this privilege to work with and learn from racialized groups and advance systemic change in educational institutions and in the larger society.

Turning our attention back to the previous section, we further highlight the relationship between identity and teacher–pupil interactions with the inclusion of Julian's revelatory disclosure: "I believe that I am the children . . . I can relate to exactly what they go through. Not because I'm walking [in] their shoes . . . specifically, but I think our experiences are kind of mirror images" (Warren et al., 2022, p. 270). In a concluding passage, this chapter expounds upon his message to illustrate how commonalities connect the various SEL competencies in the formation of an anti-racist learning environment.

As acclaimed Indigenous social critic Thomas King so wryly quips (2003), "The truth about stories is that's all we are" (p. 2). We all have stories, but as educators, what distinguishes our professional and personal stories from the rest is that—if left unexamined, and too often scarcely concealed beneath the surface of our collective consciousness—skewed narratives will continue to hold sway over our pedagogical decisions, expectations, and interactions with students and their families. Whiteness pervades every corner of the classroom atmosphere, re-creating the essence of anti-Black racism upon which much of the dehumanization of Black bodies continues to thrive. Thus, it behooves responsive anti-racist early childhood educators to confront whatever awaits in the darkness, for the light of truth reveals the specter of systemic racism and in so doing, uniquely positions the educator community to embark on an enlightening journey toward self-discovery, a process that will benefit themselves and their students.

Identity, Self-Awareness, and Social Awareness

A critical starting point in the anti-racist design process is to identify how race and racism show up in the classroom and impact children's learning. In one of the few qualitative studies on how school leaders map anti-racism onto general SEL aptitudes, Forman et al. (2022) demonstrate how participants use social–emotional strategies, such as regulation of emotions, to mitigate the emotional reactions and the resistance that may hinder the delivery of anti-racist teaching content. Building on Forman et al.'s work, but with more targeted, self-reflective questions to facilitate anti-racist professional development—including the initial conceptualization of an anti-racist early year classroom environment—we share the following queries for educators to consider:

- Am I experiencing any emotional reactions (anger, guilt, discomfort) to learning about racism, white supremacy, and systemic inequities? Consider what the underlying reasons for such emotional responses might be.
- How do I experience or express my own emotions while observing evidence of racism (racialized peer exclusion, for example)?
- Do I perpetuate a race-silenced classroom, commonly informed by colorblind ideologies (by ignoring student commentary about race and racism, or via the use of learning materials that do not reflect students' racial identities)?
- Do I provide spaces and materials that promote critical discussions about racism?
- What are my feelings about discussing race and racism with students?
- How do I communicate and build relationships with Black, Indigenous, and racialized students (and their families)? Additionally, do I center their knowledge and lived experiences in the classroom?
- Do I provide multimodal ways for children to demonstrate their learning?
- How do I approach pedagogical documentation?

Agency

Jagers et al. (2019) observe that the concept of agency "lends itself to understanding the ways in which individuals or groups employ psychological resources to express and realize resilience" (p. 170). An anti-racist framing of this dimension involves conceptualizing agency by foregrounding the equitable expressions of resistance. Thus, in the process of preparing their classrooms to receive the student body, educators should reflect on their own unique ways of resisting racialized oppression (for white educators, this may entail unpacking and/or critiquing white dominance (Mayes et al., 2022)) in keeping with a key element of the anti-racist social–emotional learning lens: critical theoretical frameworks. Familiarity with theoretical frameworks, such as Critical Race Theory (CRT), enhances educators' awareness of racism and its current significance and impact, which may in turn inform instruction, curriculum, and the selection of learning materials. Therefore, lesson plans should be scrutinized in the context of a comprehensive pedagogical analysis, along with discipline measures and teacher–student interactions. For instance, when creating a lesson plan, educators can employ the following guiding questions:

- Are the goals of the lesson grounded in anti-racist outcomes such as developing racial pride and resistance among racially and ethnically minoritized children, and anti-racist perceptions and behaviors among white children?
- Do the learning materials reflect racially and ethnically minoritized children in positive ways?
- Are your pedagogical approaches consistent with children's cultural and racial identities? For example, do you integrate artistic expressions and group learning as part of the learning process/assessment?
- Power-sharing: Have you consulted with parents to gather lived experiences and cultural knowledge that connect to the lesson in a meaningful and empowering way?

Congruent with the mission of abolitionist teaching (Love, 2019), classroom culture should likewise celebrate the ongoing legacy of resistance to inspire "creative acts of rebellion" (Sium & Ritskes, 2013) and sustain the enduring attitudes of resistance of Black and racialized groups, whether in the form of literary criticism or grassroots activism. Essentially, when children find themselves in a classroom space, they should be able to make connections to their daily lives, engage with what they are learning, and value their racial heritage(s). The structure of the classroom—as determined by the floor plans, infographics, and even the general atmosphere incorporated by the school's overall design scheme—is implicated by virtue of association in setting the tone for racialized unity (intrinsic to fostering a sense of community rooted in the shared goals of equity and justice). Consider the following questions:

- Does your classroom space reflect a diverse range of examples pertaining to anti-racism, anti-oppression, and the subversion of anti-Black racism?

- Is the classroom an empowering space that nurtures children's "freedom dreaming" (Spaulding et al, 2021), while encouraging them to envision themselves as vital participants in a communal struggle against racism and oppression?

In contemporary studies on engaging change in the lives of marginalized youth at school, data analysis reveals that racial socialization often equates with racial pride, reorienting the racially minoritized student's disposition toward one of anti-racist activism and innovation. Escayg's study on Black children's perceptions of and experiences with whiteness (2020b) identifies one participant as memorably asserting that he "would like to be the President of Equal Rights." This study showed that building and strengthening students' Afrocentric ideologies is central to anti-racist activism in the early childhood years.

The process of establishing an anti-racist classroom space prioritizes cultivating positive racial identity. Such a classroom provides examples of resistance through curriculum and activity materials; the design of the physical space is instrumental in honoring students' racial identities, developing their awareness of civil rights, agency, and supporting their participation in anti-racist individual and collective action. For instance, educators can use posters that provide a definition of resistance along with pictures that illustrate ways to stand up against racism (see Escayg, 2022). We conceptualize resistance as inspired by intergenerational accountability (reflecting on past struggles, honoring the lives and legacies of prominent activists, and demonstrating that, in fact, courageous anti-racist partnerships involve the participation of children and adults).

Anti-racist early childhood education institutes nothing short of social justice, and positively constitutes love-in-action. Such pedagogy openly and unapologetically calls into question the racist structures and performances that reinscribe white supremacy in ECE systems and spaces, thereby challenging racial, class, and gender inequities as they impinge on the lives of children. Although anti-racist teaching involves several practices, in this chapter we limited our discussion to the classroom environment, while further highlighting the importance of educators' social-emotional competencies. Even while bearing the torch of past civil rights victories, anti-racist teachers continue to blaze a collective trail by advancing inclusion and quality of life for students and their families. As we see it, the future of our humanity and the well-being of Black and racially minoritized children hang in the balance.

NOW WHAT?

An anti-racist classroom environment promotes anti-racist learning goals. At the early childhood level, these goals include cultivating a positive racial identity and developing resistance to racial ideologies that center and glorify whiteness while dehumanizing and devaluing racialized bodies and minds. As we have discussed throughout the text, however, the process begins with you, the teacher/early childhood educator: The pedagogical choices, the decisions, and the power to create an anti-racist space lie with you. So, now what can you do to begin to create an anti-bias and anti-racist classroom? In the Educators' Corner we ask you to take a look at all of the pictures, books, artwork, artifacts and anything else within the learning environment with an anti-bias and anti-racist lens to consider what all of these images are telling children about themselves and their families, communities, and cultures.

EDUCATORS' CORNER

When you next walk into your classroom, take a picture of four or five artifacts in your classroom that you imagine children will gravitate toward. Ask yourself:

- Are these items typically found in most early learning spaces? If so, why and what are their purposes?
- How do these items make learning spaces safe and joyful for Black, Hispanic, and Indigenous children and other children of color?
- How do these items strengthen Black, Latine, and Indigenous children's racial and cultural identity, if at all?
- If these items are not culturally relevant or grounded in Black, Hispanic, or Indigenous culture, consider replacing or adding four or five artifacts that speak to the cultural roots and richness of these groups and ensure that these are centered and incorporated into your curriculum and daily functioning.

CHAPTER 4

Developing a CRABAR Assessment View

Jada is a boisterous 4-year-old girl with a short ponytail adorned with colorful barrettes. At home, Jada can be found playing with her trucks and dolls, making up stories of adventures, and reading her 6-year-old brother's books. However, in class she is not vocal and does not enjoy the classroom books, and Ms. Mora, one of her preschool teachers, views Jada as angry and unengaged. Ms. Mora is worried about Jada's communication skills and motor development, and her overall "attitude." They wonder if there are problems at home that are causing Jada to be disengaged. First, Ms. Mora reaches out to Jada's mom to learn more, and through this conversation she gains a different picture of Jada. Jada's mom describes her as fun-loving and a motivated reader. Ms. Mora decides to use the standardized child learning assessment systems mandated by the district in order to get a glimpse into Jada's developmental skills.

Ms. Mora's assessment of Jada will impact her classroom placement in the district next school year. How can Ms. Mora ensure that she is providing a holistic assessment of Jada's skills that accounts for not only what she observes in the classroom but also what Jada's mother is telling her? How are the current classroom assessments and instructional practices capturing Jada's interest, knowledge and diverse ways of demonstrating this knowledge?

We now discuss how assessments that are grounded in culturally responsive, anti-bias, anti-racist (CRABAR) values can support teaching practices and continuous quality improvement to build the skills and capacity of the early childhood workforce, programs, and system-wide monitoring. We will present a framework for ensuring a culturally grounded, anti-bias, and anti-racist assessment approach. We will then check this framework to see if it aligns with current tools and provide suggestions for how existing tools can be revised or new tools created. We will break down assessments at the classroom, program, and system level, and then talk about how assessments can be used to provide information about improvements for curriculum as well as professional development.

PURPOSES OF ASSESSMENT

The purpose of assessment is to gather information that can be used to inform plans for:

- driving children's learning and healthy development,
- informing curriculum development and planning,
- shaping professional development for educators, and
- guiding policy development (resource allocation, access) and program and system accountability.

The information gathered from assessment is used to identify, interpret, and monitor trends and patterns in performance of individual children, the programs they attend, and systems that oversee these programs. Archer (2017) proposes three triangulated reasons for assessment: for learning, for certification, and for accountability. We expand and adapt Archer's view for the early childhood field by describing how assessment, when related to educating and caring for children ages birth to 5, can recast the reasoning for this triangulation to be assessment of young children's learning, assessment of classroom quality and teaching, and assessment of program quality.

Defining CRABAR Assessment

To Archer's triangulation idea we add the lens of CRABAR, which incorporates the cultural knowledge, experiences, and communication styles of children from diverse families and communities and acknowledges the social injustices, inequalities, and prejudices children face (see Figure 4.1). Such an approach also recognizes societal forces beyond the children's control that affect their growth and development, such as racism, sexism, ableism, and classism. CRABAR assessments are not only important at the child level of assessment, such as when using a test to evaluate children's individual skills, but also when considering assessment at the classroom and program level and even at the system level. Our adaptation of the Archer model emphasizes that it is important to examine all levels of assessment in order to get a whole picture: the child, classroom, and school. It is equally important to make sure that the values of anti-bias, anti-racism, and cultural responsiveness are embedded at all these levels.

Figure 4.1. CRABAR Approach of Child, Classroom, and Program Assessment

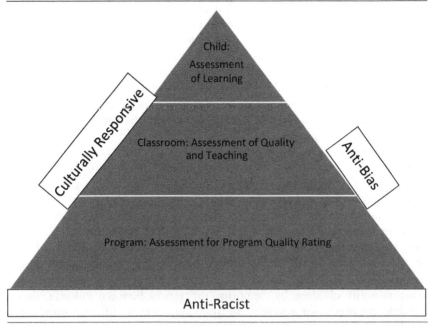

To understand an example of how this CRABAR assessment model would work, we can draw on the scenario about Ms. Mora's assessment of Jada that was described in the opening vignette of this chapter. Ms. Mora's plan to conduct the district learning assessment touches only one level of the CRABAR assessment model, the child level that is focused on the assessment of their individual skills. However, what is clear from the model is that there are two other critical levels that also need to be examined in conjunction with Jada's individual skills, and those levels provide insight into the quality of the classroom environment and how well the program is designed to educate and support students like Jada and her family. So Ms. Mora should also ask her leadership to conduct a classroom quality observation, preferably one that centers racial equity as well as quality, like the Assessing Classroom Sociocultural Equity Scale (ACSES). It is also important that Ms. Mora speak with program/school leadership about Jada, sharing her own thoughts and impressions as well as the information she learned from Jada's mom. Discussions with leaders can help teachers understand whether there are any structural, procedural, or policy aspects that can be improved in order to foster Jada's comfort and enjoyment in the classroom.

When the CRABAR approach is taken, considerations of culture and bias are examined not only within the classroom and program level, but also at the system level, and culture is taken into consideration when assessing children's outcomes. This approach is different from the manner in which assessment has traditionally been done in early childhood. Until very recently developers went through great lengths to describe their tools as "culture neutral," and they did not investigate or acknowledge the bias of teachers or assessors, or fully consider how classroom and program environments influence children's learning in diverse, potentially biased and harmful ways. For example, a classroom that is race neutral or stereotypical in imagery (e.g., Latines as farmers, Blacks as athletes, Asians as math experts) is potentially harmful by not recognizing the gifts and talents of children, especially when a racial group is viewed through negative stereotypes like lazy, unintelligent, and unworthy. In addition, stereotypical images are harmful because they limit children's opportunities to be curious and dream, and restrict children to a single view of their capacity.

In one study focused on protecting Black and minority children from harm during the child protection process, Webb and colleagues (2002) found that, first and foremost, all children have the right to be protected based on the United National Convention of Civil Rights. Second, cultural stereotypes and colorblindness can lead to the harming of Black children and other minority children by "ignoring differences between cultures, denying different needs—or accepting or applying lower or different standards" (p. 405). Furthermore, misunderstandings and stereotypes around these cultural differences can lead to inappropriate interventions, such as declining to remove an African American child who is in physical danger because of the assumption that their group's culture "believes in physical punishment" as the only discipline strategy (Pew Research Center, 2015). Yet, this is not the case because Adkison-Bradley and colleagues (2014) report that African American families use a variety of discipline strategies with "talking to children about misbehavior" being the first line of discipline. In the case of the early childhood classroom, these cultural stereotypes about discipline can be harmful to children because teachers might make the mistaken assumption that the only way to reprimand Black children is through a "harsh and firm tone," rather than fully understanding the nuances and heterogeneity of parental discipline existing in diverse ways within racial and cultural groups.

Child Assessments. The early years are a sensitive time for brain development for language, cognition, and emotion regulation (NASEM, 2019). Thus, this is a prime opportunity to provide high quality, enriching choices, experiences, and interactions for children. Child assessments can help us determine which experiences, choices, and interactions are best suited for each child's unique interests and skills. The early years are also a critical time to assess children's development. Child assessments are used for many things, including identifying children's strengths and needs, catching developmental needs, and preventing delays. It is often the first line of investigation to ensure that children's environments are meeting their needs.

> Observing, documenting, and assessing each child's development and learning are essential processes for educators and programs to plan, implement, and evaluate the effectiveness of the experiences they provide to children. Assessment includes both formal and informal measures as tools for monitoring children's progress toward a program's desired goals. Educators can be intentional about helping children to progress when they know where each child is with respect to learning goals. (NAEYC, 2020, p.19)

Assessments are important because they provide clinicians, educators, and other professionals with timely information about children's growth and development and their response to their complex environments, such as home, community, and school. Child assessments are also important for providing information about a child's nutrition, interactions with caregivers and peers, their understanding of curriculum, or their exposure to environmental toxins. For example, well baby checkup visits include an assessment, usually through a screener, to evaluate children's communication, gross motor, fine motor, problem solving, and personal-social development (Pierce et al., 2011). These developmental screening tools, such as the Ages and Stages Questionnaire-3 (ASQ-3; Squires et al., 2009; Bricker et al., 2019), are a critical part of children's assessment because they are:

- Quick to use during medical, home, or school visits, or through telemedical visits
- Accessible to diverse families (e.g., racial, ethnic, linguistic, economic level)

These assessments can:

- Capture children's strengths and milestones as well as potential areas of concerns
- Increase what parents know about their children's development, and provide information on areas that may require more extensive assessment
- Help to keep track of developmental risks that children may experience or develop over time
- Be used with diverse children (e.g., racial, ethnic, linguistic, economic level, ability).

Authentic assessment is considered best practice for the evaluation of young children, and such assessment "provides profiles of the child's strengths and needs and generates functional goals that can guide intervention planning. Simply put, authentic assessment gives a truer picture of what the children really can do and cannot do" (Bagnato et al., 2010, p. 14). Authentic assessment is developmentally appropriate to children's age and ability and is given in the context of children's familiar routines and activities and materials, such as using materials and words familiar to children (e.g., use of "soda" when some use the term "pop," asking children what a "top" toy is when they play with materials found in nature).

The fourth principle of NAEYC's statement on developmentally appropriate practice opens: "Although general progressions of development and learning can be identified, variations due to cultural contexts, experiences, and individual differences must also be considered" (NAEYC, 2020, p. 10).

What is often missing when assessments suggest being sensitive to children's diverse backgrounds is *how* to consider that, especially when many racially and minoritized backgrounds are viewed from a deficit lens. To see the *how* and the value of considering children's diverse cultural and linguistic backgrounds, let's take a look at a sample scenario that features Sherry, a speech-language pathologist, and her assessment of Carter, a preschooler whose family emigrated from Jamaica.

Sherry, a speech-language pathologist (SLP), is trying to accurately and appropriately measure the vocabulary abilities of Carter, a preschooler whose family emigrated from Jamaica at the beginning of the school year. In the intake form, the family explains that while they are fluent English speakers, they use some British English pronunciations and spellings, and the parents often speak patois when they are talking to each other or sharing stories. It is clear that Carter comes from a multilingual home environment. However, the SLP overlooks these nuances and marks that the child is a monolingual English speaker. She proceeds to administer a standardized vocabulary assessment that was normed on samples of children from within the United States.

Reflection Questions:

- What potential problems do you see happening with Carter's performance on the assessment? What are the implications for how Carter's language may be viewed by teachers if they fail to acknowledge his multilingual heritage?

- How might bias about Black people who emigrate from English-speaking countries influence Sherry failing to recognize Carter, a Black child, as multilingual?
- What else could the parents do to make sure that Sherry understands that their child is multilingual?

The National Institute of Early Education Research's (NIEER) *State of Preschool Yearbook 2017* has a specific metric related to child assessment that is encompassed in their first benchmark: *Early Learning and Development Standards (ELDS)*. In this first benchmark the focus is on expectations and alignment for children's development across multiple domains, including physical well-being and motor development, social–emotional development, approaches toward learning, language development, and cognition and general knowledge. In order for pre-kindergarten programs to meet this benchmark, they must be "aligned with any required child assessments, and sensitive to children's diverse cultural and language backgrounds" (Friedman-Krauss et al., 2018, p. 17).

Classroom Assessment. Use of assessments is one of the markers to determine whether an early childhood program is high quality. According to the National Association of Education of Young Children (NAEYC, 2020), high-quality learning environments are those in which a teacher uses a curriculum to guide children's learning and assessments to examine children's learning and growth. The classroom is the one key space where a lot of information is being received and shared that impacts children's development, learning, and well-being. That is, classrooms are the vehicles that transmit, translate, and create different pathways for children's development and learning over time. Classrooms are the place where programs', schools', and arguably, society's, rules and expectations are communicated. Beyond academic skills, classrooms are also where children learn to work with others, manage their emotions, negotiate their identity, and so much more. Unfortunately, too many studies show that Black children and other children of color, multilingual and multidialectal children, and children with disabilities do not have equal access to opportunities to learn.

In one of her seminal pieces, Linda Darling-Hammond (1998) notes, "Educational outcomes for minority children are much more a function of their unequal access to key educational resources, including skilled teachers and quality curriculum, than they are a function of race. In fact, the U.S. educational system is one of the most unequal in the industrialized world, and students routinely receive dramatically different learning opportunities based on their social status" (p. 1). In fact, data indicates that the quality of instruction received by Black children, is on average, of lower quality compared to other children (Dobbins et al., 2016; Iruka et al., 2022). For example, in one early childhood study of pre-K programs across the country, Early and colleagues (2010) found that classes with more Black and Hispanic children and children from low income households were less enriching and stimulating and had more didactic instruction, meaning one-way talking from teachers to children, "drill and kill," less time for hearing children's perspectives, and more rigidity and control of children's movement and language, compared to classrooms with fewer Black and Hispanic children. This research is not presented as an indictment of the early childhood workforce, but rather as a reminder about how high quality learning experiences are rationed by race.

Unfortunately, children's opportunities to learn can be clouded by teacher attitudes, beliefs, or biases about children based on their race (Ford & Moore, 2013; Tenenbaum & Ruck, 2007). Implicit bias in the classroom impacts whether a child is viewed as curious versus talkative or precocious versus defiant, and receives preferential treatment and positive interactions, and high expectation. In their study with early childhood educators, Blackson and colleagues (2022) found that ECE teachers were more likely than teachers at the elementary, middle, and high school levels to say there was no racism in their field, and to self-report that they ascribed to a "colorblind" approach to teaching, meaning they reported not having any racial preference among students. However, their scores on the Implicit Attitudes Test (IAT), a marker of unconscious attitudes that can influence behaviors, indicated that the majority of teachers held pro-white/anti-Black bias, and this was especially the case for white teachers. Thus, classrooms are places where white supremacy values and ideology are being transmitted, oppressing the value, culture, and contribution of Black, Indigenous, Latine, and other communities of color.

USING A CRABAR LENS FOR ASSESSMENT OF CLASSROOM QUALITY

Most well-known classrooms assessments, such as the Classroom Assessment Scoring System (CLASS) and the Environment Rating Scales (ERS), were not created with an CRABAR lens to ensure that they are free from bias and culturally grounded in the strengths of minoritized children and communities, and that learning opportunities, instruction, and the environment work for all children, especially for children who are from historically marginalized communities. We must recognize that assessment of classrooms using CRABAR also requires a critically conscious analysis of teachers' pedagogical approaches. Taking a CRABAR approach to classroom and teaching assessment must include the following (adapted from Lee (2012) of Edutopia):

- **Discussion about race and racism.** Evaluate the extent to which race is not ignored, but rather allowed to be openly discussed in a positive and affirming way, especially when addressing and discussing unspoken biases evident in society (e.g., Black people are poor and good at athletics, Hispanic people are all undocumented and good cooks). Ignoring how race is created, stratified, and reified in our classroom structure and materials does not move us toward social justice teaching. Arguably, the colorblind approach has maintained and continued the disparities seen in so many learning spaces, including early education. More importantly, these practices of ignoring race are harmful for children who are irrevocably harmed, especially our racially and ethnically diverse children, families, and workforce.
- **Connection with community organizations and members.** It is important that educators are able to identify the cultural assets of communities and members of those communities and not view communities through a white, middle-class privilege lens. For example, find out from the community leaders and elders what the community is like and how they connect with each other, help each other in a time of need, and support children. Being able to see communities through authentic and continuous interaction will help to dispel long-held harmful tropes.
- **Recognition of the diversity of racially and ethnically minoritized communities.** While racial groups have many shared experiences, languages, customs, and traditions, as well as shared oppression, dehumanization, and harm, it is important to explore the diversity within racial and ethnic groups; they are not a monolith. Black and brown communities differ in their country of origin, language and dialect, family structure, and socioeconomic status, and so much more. This means that REM children's individual identity, family, and community must be authentically recognized and incorporated into the classroom. For example, think about the story of Carter presented earlier. Carter lived in a multilingual household, rather than an English-only household, which is often assumed for Black children. Sherry's bias assumptions impeded her ability to do an accurate assessment of Carter's skills.

    Similarly, this mistaken assumption about the lack of heterogeneity (differences among groups) is evident when talking about or when describing Native American/Alaska Native groups. Yet there are 574 federally recognized Indian Nations (also called tribes, bands, pueblos, communities, and native villages) in the United States, all with their own culture, traditions, and language (National Congress of American Indians, 2020). There are also state-recognized tribes, which may be the different from the federal tribes. Nevertheless, each nation has its own tribal governance, political relationship with the federal government, and more importantly, customs, traditions, and language.

- **Represent a diversity of information.** Reading is Fundamental (RIF), a well-known campaign slogan and organization founded in 1966, is focused on providing literacy opportunities for children. While RIF is targeted to children, it is important as well for teachers to not only teach reading to readers, but also teach students to be critically conscious change agents who are exposed to historical and contemporary information on how racism and bias operate in society and the classroom. The sources can be books or other resources and professional development materials offering factual information and tools to fully love and educate children (see recommended Resources List).
- **Encourage educators to become self-aware of bias.** Classroom culture is a living and breathing organism that is influenced by adults and children. However, as leaders of this learning space, educators are in a powerful position to set the tone. This can only start with educators being aware of their biases and how they may operate in classrooms, practices, and learning opportunities.
- **Contain self-reflection activities.** Examine whether discipline practices, conversation turns (or time spent talking back and forth), praise, positive affirmation and affection, high expectations, and movement of body are influenced by children's demographic identity, such as their race, gender, language, and ability status. You can do this by keeping a checklist each day of who you spend time talking to and helping in class. On this sheet you should also note those children who seem to always be close to you (e.g., they sit next to you on the rug, or they are always willing to give you a hug).

THEY'RE NOT TOO YOUNG TO TALK ABOUT RACE

Look at the graphic here: http://www.childrenscommunityschool.org/wp-content/uploads/2018/02/theyre-not-too-young-1.jpg and ask yourself the following:

- What skills do you notice happening at each age?
- Have you seen examples of these in your classroom?

- Were you surprised to learn that children begin to notice race or skin color so young?
- At what age should educators and adults begin to talk about race and racism with children?
- What can you do to prepare yourself to engage in these conversations?

Given the information provided in this graphic, it is clear that children are capable of understanding race and racism. But what do educators do when children begin to ask those tough questions about race that even we as adults sometimes cannot answer? Some experts provide advice on how to address these questions.

Read: "Experts answer your kid's tough questions about race and racism: *What to say when your student asks why police are mean to Black people, and other questions*" (Mader, 2020; see also http://www.childrenscommunity school.org/wp-content/uploads/2018/02/theyre-not-too-young-1.jpg).

Assessment of Systems. As noted previously, use of assessments is one of the markers used to determine whether an early childhood program is high quality. There are several ways in which programs are assessed and attention to CRABAR is only beginning to be considered. For example, the Head Start Program Performance Standards are used to assess the quality and compliance of all Head Start programs within the United States and its territories. Many states use a Quality Rating Improvement System (QRIS) to assess the quality and compliance of all the licensed early childhood programs within the state.

In the Head Start Program Performance Standards (see Table 4.1), quality ranking is based on evidence that programs are meeting the performance areas, including governance, program operations, financial and administrative requirements, and federal administrative procedures (U.S. Department of Health and Human Services, Administration for Children & Families, 2021). Within each domain, there are specific foci. For example, within program operations, the focus on education and child development program services assesses the quality of the learning environment, curricula, child screening and assessments, parent and family engagement in education and child development services, and language preservation and revitalization. Thus, the standards go beyond basic health and safety standards to program operations and governance.

Quality rating and improvement systems were established to improve quality of program regardless of setting (e.g., school, center, home), funder (e.g., Head Start, education, subsidy), and auspice (e.g., school system, nonprofit). QRIS seeks to rate what quality is and most indicators include

Table 4.1. Head Start Program Performance Standards

Standards	Focus
Governance	Focused on a formal structure for a policy council at the agency level, a policy committee at the delegate level, and a parent committee. These governing bodies have a legal and fiscal responsibility to administer and oversee the Head Start and Early Head Start programs; policy councils are responsible for the direction of the Head Start and Early Head Start programs.
Program Operations	Eligibility, recruitment, selection, enrollment, and attendance (ERSEA); Program structure (e.g., center-based, home-based, locally designed variation); education and child development program services (e.g., learning environment, curricula, child screening and assessments, parent and family engagement in education and child development services, language preservation and revitalization); health program services (e.g., child health status and care, oral health practices, child nutrition, child mental health, family support services); family and community engagement services (e.g., family and community partnership services, family engagement); services for children with disabilities (e.g., inclusion, services for children and families, coordination and collaboration with local agency implementing IDEA); transition services (e.g., transition from programs to kindergarten, transition between programs); services to enrolled pregnant women (e.g., prenatal and postpartum information and services, family partnership services); human resources management (e.g., personnel policies, staff qualifications and competency requirements, training and PD, staff health and wellness); program management and quality improvement (e.g., program goals assessment, management system)
Financial and Administrative Requirements	Non-federal match; administrative requirements such as insurance and bonding, protection for the privacy of child records such as disclosures and parental rights; delegation of program operations such as establishing and monitoring delegate agencies; facilities, including attending to purchasing, renovating, and maintaining facilities; transportation, including vehicle safety operation and procedures
Federal Administrative Procedures	Processes that ensure programs meet performance standards and have grants open for competition; ERSEA, program structure, education, health, family and community engagement, human resources and professional development, program management, and administrative fiscal requirements

Source. U.S. Department of Health and Human Services, Administration for Children & Families (2021).

environment, curriculum, professional development and staff qualifications, and program administration, and to a lesser extent, parent engagement (Lugo-Gil et al., 2011; Porter et al., 2011). As noted by Meek and colleagues (2022):

> Though these systems [QRIS] have the potential to advance equity in early care and education systems, thus far, they have fallen short. They have rightly been criticized by advocates for being exclusive, rather than inclusive, leaving out lower-resourced providers, providers of color, and home-based or family child care providers, in effect disadvantaging or locking them out altogether of opportunities to receive state resources, both financial—through tiered systems of reimbursement—and coaching and professional development resources. (p. 3)

QRIS has been accused of being racist in purpose, function, and outcomes. One such charge came in 2020, when early childhood professionals in California opened a protest with the bold statement, "*QRIS is racist*" (Nzewi et al., 2020). While policy makers have been discussing for years how QRIS can be used to ensure cultural responsiveness, issues of racial equity and bias have not been fully interrogated and examined in how QRIS defines and operationalizes quality (Meek et al., 2022). The goal of QRIS is to monitor programs for quality and be able to be used to predict child outcomes. While QRIS has been successfully used as a monitoring system, research has shown that many of the structural indicators were not predictive of child outcomes. However, process quality as measured by the CLASS *was* predictive of child outcomes (Sabol et al., 2013), and even more so process quality with a focus on racial equity measured by ACSES is also predictive of child outcomes (Curenton et al, 2022).

BUILD is one of the leading policy and advocacy organizations in the early childhood field. It is, in fact, the very organization that championed and scaled QRIS across the country. At BUILD's national conference in 2022, the question was raised as to how to build systems of quality that advance equity. One pair of invited presenters, Etter and Capizzano (2022), describe their work with states that reports that their experience with QRIS. They found that that approximately 80% of programs run by providers who are Black, Indigenous, Latine, and from other communities of color receive one-star ratings, and 77% of REM children were attending such low-rated programs. Thus, they argue the current QRIS system fails to fit the view we proposed of adopting CRABAR principles.

In fact, Etter and Capizzano (2022) articulate how the QRIS system is based upon dominant, white cultural narratives, and artifacts used to maintain historical systems of power and wealth and ignore or justify racial inequalities. They explain how the white cultural values of individualism, "one right way," and paternalism are represented in the QRIS system respectively as program ratings and rewards that are the foundation for resource distribution, quality standards based upon a white dominant standard, and compliance measures that maintain the power structure of some programs being at the top and others at the bottom. Differences in star ratings across programs are supposed to be based on a program's individual efforts, determination, and dedication, and these programs are then rewarded for their efforts. However, it is not fully acknowledged that these rating differences are due to inequalities in access to resources and foundational issues related to systemic inequality. Programs with more access to resourses are able to harness them for their quality improvement efforts, which are then rewarded by the system. This produces an even greater gap between the quality ratings of the programs.

In order to create a CRABAR system level assessment, several things have got to change. First and foremost, fostering racial equity in terms of children's access to programs, program financing, and parental influence has to become central to the mission of QRIS. Second, the definition of quality needs to be redefined to include more cultural representations of what quality is and how best children learn. Third, the power structures associated with QRIS needs to be dismantled and resources need to be redistributed. For example, instead of rewarding programs with incentives if they have more stars, the QRIS system should start to invest in those programs that have fewer stars. This aligns with Etter and Capizzano's (2022) three big ideas for rebuilding the QRIS: (1) eliminate many of the QRIS indicators that are not predictive of child outcomes and instead focus on teacher-child interactions done in different ways (2) move away from quality incentives and focus on quality investments that provide adequate funding to the workforce and programs, and (3) get rid of ratings and focus on programs identifying and showcasing their specializations (e.g., outdoor learning, dual language learning, infant-toddler care).

EDUCATORS' CORNER

The selection of evaluation assessment tools can be a confusing task, especially because you might feel pressured to maintain the status quo and use traditional measures that have commonly been used for quality and program monitoring. There might even be confusion around whether or not you actually have the autonomy to choose child outcome measures that go beyond the traditional academic-related assessments and use assessments that take a deeper look at children's social-emotional development and health.

When embarking on assessment, there are several sets of questions you should ask yourself:

- **What is the purpose and goal of the assessment?** What is the goal of the assessment? Will the results of the assessment produce answers to the questions you have about how children learn, the quality of the classroom, or how the program is functioning?
- **Does the assessment allow for inquiry at all levels of the assessment model?** From whom will you be collecting the information? Is there any information being collected about the classroom and the program's structure or operation? Are only child assessments being used? Do the child-level assessments measure all areas of children's development? Is there any information collected from parents?
- **How will the results of the assessment be used?** What will you do with the results? Can the results from the measure be easily interpreted by staff and stakeholders? How will you share and activate the results?
- **Does the assessment adopt a CRABAR approach?** Does the assessment process consider the cultural assets of children and families and the financial diversity of programs?

If the answer to any of these questions is no, then you should go back and refine the assessment approach particularly as it relates to that aspect. For example, if, when preparing for the assessment, you realize that parental input is not part of the assessment procedure, then you want to refine the approach so that parental voice and engagement are included.

EMERGING CRABAR ASSESSMENTS

The field is now beginning to actively discuss the need for assessments that consider culture and bias, and there are new tools that are emerging. For instance, at the classroom level an assessment tool that shows much promise is the Assessing Classroom Sociocultural Equity Scale (ACSES) (Curenton et al., 2019). ACSES was designed to examine classroom quality from the lens of racial equity, meaning that it not only considers the traditional features of quality like language interactions, accommodations for children with differing abilities, and children's participation, but also it considers whether teachers' instructional acts are targeted to children who are ethnically and racially diverse and whether these children are targets for harsh discipline. ACSES also considers whether or not ethnically and racially diverse children feel comfortable in the classroom environment and their connections with peers. ACSES has been used in preschool to Grade 5 classrooms (with a possibility for infant and toddler programs and classrooms), and findings across various studies indicate that when teachers have higher ACSES scores, there is a positive association with children's social–emotional and academic outcomes (Curenton et al., 2019). These findings indicate that it does matter when teachers use CRABAR practices in their teaching because such practices are related to positive outcomes for children.

A program level measure of CRABAR that is in the development phase is the Culturally Responsive Anti-Bias Anti-Racist (CRABAR) Curriculum Audit Tool (Curenton & Franco, 2022). This measure can be used by program leaders, and teachers themselves, to evaluate whether the curriculum that is currently being used in their program adopts the principles of cultural responsiveness and of being anti-bias and anti-racist. A prior version of this measure was used to examine the curriculum created by the Children's Literacy Initiative (CLI), and it has continued to be revised and expanded to be able to evaluate all preschool and early elementary curriculum. Furthermore, future iterations of the audit tool will be grounded in the theoretical model proposed by Curenton and colleagues (2022) that specifically evaluates literacy materials and activities for how well they integrate emotional literacy and racial literacy and whether the literacy materials consist of racially affirming storybooks (for examples, see lists curated by the Center on the Ecology of Early Development at https://www.bu-ceed.org/uploads/1/3/3/0/133043669/tps _booklist.pdf). The model proposes that CRABAR storybooks and curricula can be used to prompt conversations related to ethnic-racial socialization, and during such repeated and frequent conversations children begin to develop a positive ethnic-racial identity and better emotional skills, which in turn leads to children having racial literacy skills (Stevenson, 2014).

A third emerging assessment is one that can be used to measure the social capital and cultural wealth of REM families. Such a measure has been used in a national study of early childhood well-being, the RAPID-EC Project (https://rapidsurveyproject.com). The Rapid Assessment of Pandemic Impact on Development in Early Childhood (RAPID-EC) project is an early childhood family well-being survey designed to gather essential information in a continuous manner regarding the needs, health-promoting behaviors, and well-being of children and their families during the coronavirus (COVID-19) outbreak in the United States. The Family Cultural Wealth Survey (Iruka et al., 2022a) asks caregivers of young children to report on various cultural events and traditions, support networks, and social media connection and advocacy. In Table 4.2, we provide definitions of family cultural assets and how each asset may be exhibited by children.

While everyone, regardless of race, culture, and other social identities, can relate to many of these assets, preliminary evidence indicates that Black

Table 4.2. Cultural Wealth Area and Definition

	Definition	Example of how asset may be exhibited or experienced by children
Aspirational Capital	Ability to maintain hopes and dreams for the future, even in the face of real and perceived barriers	The child who is working to be able to swing high on the swing, or write their name or be able to say a word, especially when they are being told that they can't do it.
Linguistic Capital	Intellectual and social skills attained through communication experiences in more than one language and/or style	The child who translates things for their parents or the child who code switches; these are communication experiences that require intellect and social skills. Think about the storytelling that children are exposed to, which helps build their memory, language, visualization, attention to details, and flair. This can happen through different mediums: art, music, and poetry.
Familial Capital	Cultural knowledges nurtured among familial kin that carry a sense of community history, memory, and cultural intuition	Bonds of extended family (living or passed), blood or nonbiological, that help children connect to their community and cultural roots. This allows children to understand that there are many besides their parents who care for them and will protect them, including childcare providers and educators.
Social Capital	Networks of people and community resources. These peer and other social contacts can provide both instrumental and emotional support to navigate through society's institutions	Resources such as families who reach out to their neighbors or church folks for help with child care, finances, and emotional support. What, or who, are children's social capital: peers whom they feel close to, friends who help them relax if they are scared or angry? Who is their joyful friend?
Navigational Capital	Skills of maneuvering through social institutions	What children do when they need to navigate through situations; they may want a hug to get out of a jam, they may lash out if they are feeling uncomfortable. What skills does that Black boy bring to deal with the fact that he may be viewed as the bad or scary kid? Does he often say please or thank you, or try to do other things like sit down rather than stand up so he is not seen as the big kid?

(continued)

Table 4.2. (continued)

	Definition	Example of how asset may be exhibited or experienced by children
Resistant Capital	Knowledge and skills fostered through oppositional behavior that challenges inequality	What many kids do when they are bold about how much they love themselves. They talk about what they did at home or why they like the food their parents make, especially when they get a sense that something about them may not be viewed as positive.
Perseverant Capital	Skills to cope with obstacles and adversities	For a child who may be the only kid with a disability, who speaks a different language or sounds different, continuing to try to tie their shoe, or coming back persistently to the word or work they struggled with.
Spiritual Capital	Beliefs, knowledge, values, and dispositions that drive societal, organizational and interpersonal behavior (as defined by the Spiritual Capital & Moral Leadership Institute: https://scmli.com/what-is-spiritual-capital/)	Resources that families rely on and pass down to their children that can build moral character, including empathy for other people; many families may also rely on faith-based institutions for social and economic resources, including hope for the future, protection from poverty and inhumane experiences, and for material support (e.g., food, shelter, clothing).

people and other racially and ethnically marginalized groups are likely to report using these assets to cope with a racialized society. As stated by Yosso (2005), "A traditional view of cultural capital is narrowly defined by White, middle-class values, and is more limited than wealth—one's accumulated assets and resources. . . . Centering the . . . lens on the experiences of People of Color in critical historical context reveals accumulated assets and resources in the histories and lives of Communities of Color" (p. 77). It is important that we move beyond the deficit views of racial and ethnic minorities to one that sees their assets beyond their individually "accumulated assets and resources (i.e., ownership of stocks, money in bank, real estate, business ownership, etc.)" (Yosso, 2005, p. 77).

Now it is your turn to think about how these cultural assets show up in your life and how they can show in up in how you assess children, especially children with multiple marginalized social identities (e.g., race, gender, class, disability, language).

REFLECTION ACTIVITY

Focus on one of the eight cultural wealth definitions:

Aspirational Capital
Linguistic Capital
Familial Capital
Social Capital
Navigational Capital
Resistant Capital
Perseverant Capital
Spiritual Capital

Think about which one connects the most with you.

Why did you pick this one?
How does this show up in your behavior and your work?
How was this asset formed?

Then think about how that asset can be used as a lens when you are working with families.

Think about the family of one of your students: What type of capital
do you see respresented in their family?
What can you learn from this family?
How can you help this family gain access to even more capital?

NOW WHAT?

We have been describing the importance of assessment within the school and classroom, but it is important to think about assessment that happens outside of the school as well, especially when such an assessment provides an opportunity to hear the voice of parents. Iruka, Curenton, and Eke (2014) wrote a book, *The CRAF-E4 Family Engagement Model*, which talked about taking a CRABAR approach to family engagement. We discussed this in Chapter 2. In the book, the authors encourage school personnel to go through the 4Es process: Exploration, Expectation, Education, and Empowerment.

Exploration. REM children and their families have a rich set of resources and skills that demand to be explored and valued. There is a rich history of spirituality, collectivism, and "stick-to-it-iveness" that many families give to their child, and this needs to be explored. Families are a rich source of information about children's skills, abilities, competencies, and capacities that can help contextualize and interpret what educators see in the classroom. For example, Jada not liking the books in the classrooms may be due to her preferring different kinds of books that may keep her engaged. However, this information may not come out without connecting with the families and exploring children's behaviors, especially those that may be viewed as problematic. While parents may have a different view of their children than teachers do, their perspectives are still critical. Educators can find out how families and their children have been doing, especially with traumatic events like pandemic, shootings, unforeseen weather calamity, etc. Educators can ask parents if they have noticed changes in their children: Do they find them reading more, talking more, sharing their emotions, treating younger siblings and peers more gently, or coming back to a task or activity after failures and frustrations? Educators can also invite parents to observe in the classroom and debrief with parents afterwards, which can be part of the assessment document. The assessment of children needs to examine their environment, including their home, school, and community environments. Home visits are great way to understand what children experience in their home and outside their home in their communities. When teachers meet with families in their homes, they not only see cultural and linguistic customs and patterns, but they may see how children engage and navigate in their home environment (e.g., seeing a child feed his baby brother, or get their mother's hair scarf).

Expectation. We know that expectation is one of a few factors found to be predictive of many child outcomes over time (Fantuzzo et al., 2004; Iruka et al., 2018). Expectations matter because once you have high expectations you will create the conditions so children can meet these expectations. As you think about assessments, consider whether they will provide an authentic representation of children's skills and provide multiple avenues for showing development and being right. Are these truly capturing children's skills or what you expect of them? For example, does the assessment allow children to show their learning through fine and gross motor skills rather than verbal? Is credit given when children use different language systems or dialects?

Education. Due to the history of disenfranchisement of REM children, especially Black and Indigenous children, from high-quality education, it is paramount that we are providing opportunities for high-order thinking and learning rather than things that require rote memory. We need children to be in spaces where they get to explore their thinking about how the world works. Education needs to go beyond basic facts and discrete knowledge to critical thinking and problem solving. Dr. Gloria Ladson-Billings (1995) notes that culturally relevant teaching must ensure students (1) experience academic success, (2) develop and/or maintain cultural competence, and (3) develop critical consciousness. This means that assessment should examine where children show promise and excellence, how connected children feel to their culture and heritage, and how much critical thinking are they engaging in during activities and conversations (e.g., why is that bird blue, why are Juan and Jeremiah on the other side of the room?).

Empowerment. When it comes to empowerment when working with families, it is important to understand the essence of empowerment means the active and conscious "relinquishing of power" by the dominant group (Page & Czuba, 1999). The crux of all early care and education is to endow children with the skills, mindset, and resources to support their engagement in the learning and schooling enterprise, and educators and school leaders cannot do this without being willing to give up the power that has been unjustly bestowed upon them due to their position as leaders of the school (Page & Czuba, 1999). This power takes on the form of being seen as the "experts" in children's learning and development or as "having ultimate and final authority" over what happens in schools and how children are treated in school. Yet, empowerment is meant to cause those in power to question and challenge our assumptions and how social systems operate. We must ensure children (and families) are able to activate their strength, confidence, and the know-how to control their life and claim their rights. Empowerment can take many forms: economic, cultural, or political. However, in the context of our work, we are focused on empowering families to be liberators, meaning ensuring families and children have the supports and resources they need in order to activate their endowed strength, confidence, and know-how to maximize their education. Liberation only happens when those who traditionally hold power, such as teachers or school leaders, relinquish some of their power and create the conditions for parents and children to step up and demonstrate their skills, ideas, and assets. Liberation needs trust that those who will fill the void have what is needed to speak their own truths, make decisions on behalf of themselves, and advocate for their own needs. We can create the condition for children and families to be empowered and ready to deal with all of what schools (and society) throw at them, from academic to social challenges, by engaging in interactions with families that are grounded in the CRABAR approach.

HOW ASSESSMENTS SHOULD BE USED

Assessments, regardless of whether they are formative or summative, should be used to equip educators with information on children's strengths as well as the areas that need more attention. And educators have to be ready, and know how to share this information with families in a manner that builds children's confidence, skills, and knowledge base, and it is especially critical that children are not being assessed through a lens of whiteness that erases their cultural assets (e.g., child needs speech therapy because they speak African American English or Spanglish). What resources do you need to authentically assess children to support their learning? Do the summative assessments given to children (e.g., DIBELS) capture the skills and talents of children, especially REM children? Are the observations of children based on their full selves or based on their distance from white normative expectation (e.g., their language or dialect, how they play, their tone)?

In sum, the CRABAR assessment approach we proposed moves beyond the constant comparison of REM versus white children (Gardner-Neblett et al., 2021; Ford et al, 2001). It is also important for us to move assessment beyond Eurocentric standards of quality and best practice. Instead, as a field, we need to address the root cause of racially skewed assessment outcomes, which is disparity due to structural racism. This means that assessment of children is incomplete if it does not consider environments and contexts such as the classroom and program. In fact, it is also important to examine external factors in the communities and intergenerational factors (e.g., lead exposure, trauma, adverse childhood experiences) as well. Recognizing that not all external factors can always be considered, it is important that children's assessments, especially assessments of Black and Latine children, are examined through a racialized lens that recognizes the intergenerational impact and foundation of racism and dehumanization while also balancing the need to identify the strengths and skills that children bring to the learning context alongside areas that need strengthening.

CHAPTER 5

Valuing the Early Childhood Workforce to Sustain CRABAR Practices

Education is our passport to the future, for tomorrow belongs to the people who prepare for it today.

—Malcolm X

Ms. Corcoran has been a home-based childcare owner and provider for over 25 years. She has cared for and taught over a thousand children in her lifetime. Much of her evenings, weekends, and holidays are given up to make sure her home meets the state, county, and city health and safety regulations, and the curriculum meets the needs of her diverse and active children. Her communication with parents is clear and consistent (often having to find a way to translate information for parents who don't speak English), finding where to get extra diapers, formula, and nutritious foods, and going to the local libraries and book hubs to find books and classroom supplies since the resources she is given by the state and city are not what her children enjoy most. She had to pick up a side job as a school tutor to help cover the expenses of her ECE business, especially when parents are not always able to pay the child care fees. Despite the demands, she enjoys her work with children and believes teaching children is her life's work and mission.

Individuals in this profession hold hands and books, wipe tables and noses, talk and listen, care for injuries and classroom walls, manage disputes and varied standards, discover new bugs and ways to tie shoes, but most importantly, what they do is give lessons on reading, writing, arithmetic, and life. Many of them are also working multiple fronts, including being a pseudo-therapist and social worker for families and giving families breaks on child care fees, including taking money out of their pocket to feed, enrich, and clothe the children in their care. These individuals whom we call social justice warriors (Iruka et al., 2020) are also the brain-building workforce, deserving of reverence, gratitude, awe, value, protection, and compensation. Unfortunately, the treatment, protection, and compensation of early educators seldom reach the high levels they deserve, and their professional standards, including qualifications and competencies often doesn't quite meet quality benchmarks.

THE VAST ROLE AND LIMITED COMPENSATION
FOR ECE PROFESSIONALS

According to the 2020 Early Childhood Workforce Index, the average annual pay for child care workers is $24,230 ($11.65/hr), $30,520 for preschool teachers ($14.67/hr) compared to $48,210 ($23.18) for center directors and $56,850 ($32.80) for kindergarten teachers. ECE professionals face a pay penalty for working with young children, meaning that even with a bachelor's degree, ECE professionals have a higher chance of living in poverty compared to K–8 teachers (McLean et al., 2021). For example, the poverty rate for ECE educators in New Mexico is 27.4% compared to 4.1% for K–8 teachers, which amounts to a 50.6% pay penalty for early childhood educators. The pay penalty for ECE educators with a bachelor's degree is 37.8% in California, 2.9% in Florida, 35% in Massachusetts, and 22% in Wyoming. Large or small, there is a pay penalty in every state in the Union!

Racial disparities in compensation also exist within the ECE profession. Black early educators are paid, on average, $0.78 less per hour than their White peers. The pay gap is more than doubled for Black educators who work with preschool-age children ($1.71 less per hour compared with their White peers) compared with the pay gap for Black educators who work with infants and toddlers ($0.77 less per hour compared with their White peers)" (McLean et al., 2021, p. 40). This means that Black ECE professionals are bound to lose about $1,622.40 per year if they choose to work with preschool age children. Furthermore, center-based Black early educators are less likely to earn $15 per hour than all other racial/ethnic groups in the early education workforce nationwide, even after controlling for education attainment (Austin et al., 2019). Workforce economic data suggest that there is a 16 cent wage gap between Black female teachers and their white teacher colleagues which over the course of a person's career could equate to a significant lost in wealth and economic mobility (Whitebook et al., 2018).

These low and inequitable wages means that ECE professionals will likely experience material and financial hardship. For example, a majority of ECE professionals qualify for Supplemental Nutrition Assistance (SNAP) benefits. This means their income is below $26,124. As noted by Lloyd and colleagues (2021), due to the low pay coupled with limited employer benefits (e.g., health insurance, retirement savings, paid sick leave, vacation), many ECE professionals qualify for public benefits.

Fisher's (2021) RAPID-EC Child Care Provider Survey found that:

- One in four child care providers reported having at least one other job, and over 40% of them reported that providing child care accounted for less than half of their income.
- One in three child care providers has experienced at least one material hardship (e.g., food, housing, utilities) during the pandemic.
- Family/friend/neighbor (FFN) providers reported significantly more material hardship (43.8%) than providers in center-based (32.6%) or home-based (32.9%) child care settings.
- When child care providers' material hardship increased so did their emotional distress. (Fisher, 2021).

LOW AND INEQUITABLE WAGES FOR ECE PROFESSIONALS EXPLAINED BY LEGACY OF RACISM AND SEXISM

Many people lament: Why is the ECE workforce treated so poorly? Why can't they be valued, professionally respected, and compensated fairly? They are so important to our economy, and they deserve so much more. Unfortunately, the long reach of enslavement and racism intersecting with sexism still touches today's ECE workforce. For centuries, paid domestic service work has been viewed as the domain of women of color (Vogtman, 2017). Enslaved women were the primary caregivers for their enslavers' children. They provided care and teaching for white children, while their own children were denied their full attention. Even after enslaved people were free, the only positions many women were able to get, especially in the South, were as housekeepers and child care providers. As historian Claudia Goldin observes, "Black women had been abundantly represented in the labor market as slaves and . . remained so as freed persons" (quoted in Vogtman, 2017).

Many women of color have been trained to serve white people, families, and communities. For instance, Black women were trained in domestic skills in higher education institutions such as Spelman college to work on behalf of white people and their families. In the Southwest, predominantly Mexican and Mexican American women did provide domestic and childcare work (de la Liz Ibarra, 2000). In the West, Japanese women are overwhelmingly represented within the early childhood and domestic workforce (Mendoza, 2001). There is also a history of Indigenous girls and young women being taken from their homes and forced to do domestic labor for white families (Jacobs, 2008).

Persistent gender stereotypes have also depressed pay for women and the jobs in which they predominate—especially ECE jobs (Vogtman, 2017). Jobs in which women predominate, including child care, nurse's aide, and housekeepers, are viewed as invisible and not worthy of pay or even protection. For example, janitors and building cleaners do the same thing as maids and housekeepers, but they are paid at least 10% higher because those jobs are male dominated (Stearns, 2012). Thus, it is not a surprise that child care workers continue to be one of the lowest-paid occupations nationwide. When all occupations are ranked by annual pay, child care workers remain nearly at the bottom (McLean et al., 2021). Preschool teachers and directors of child care centers or preschools are also subject to low wages, particularly compared with teachers of school-age children.

Federal (and state) child care policy has reflected and contributed to the continuing devaluation of the ECE sector and its professionals. During the global COVID-19 pandemic, businesses were having difficulty retaining their employees and were not able to return to their normal pre-pandemic levels, in large part due to limited access to childcare for their workforce. As a result, national, state and local governments and agencies began to consider the impact limited access to childcare was having on the overall economy and individuals returning to the workforce. As a result, there was an increase in the momentum and interest among policy officials and education leaders to shore up the ECE sector and the workforce. In particular the Biden Administration's Build Back Better Framework began to prioritize early childhood workforce compensation (The White House, 2021a). This framework invested in children, families, and caregivers, including the ECE workforce, through its provision for preschool for all children and expansion of access to high-quality care for children, which would have brought an infusion of funds to the ECE sector to adequately compensate and provide necessary benefits for many ECE professions.

Rather than address the ECE infrastructure as expected, a smaller and scaled back infrastructure bill was passed in August 2022 called the Inflation Reduction Act. The Inflation Reduction Act focuses on health care (i.e., cutting prescription drug costs, lowering health care costs), clean energy (i.e., lower energy costs, building clean energy infrastructure, reducing pollution) and taxes (i.e., taxing high earning corporations, reducing deficit). Again, although the ECE sector has been proven to be a critical U.S. infrastructure, it has once again been ignored in policy and community investment. There have been many instances in our nation's history where child care was positioned to be treated as a human right for all, though its origination as the domain of women, especially enslaved women, still served as a backdrop (see the textbox for a brief history adapted from Vogtman, 2017, and Figure 5.1).

Figure 5.1. Federal Policy on Child Care, 1900-2022

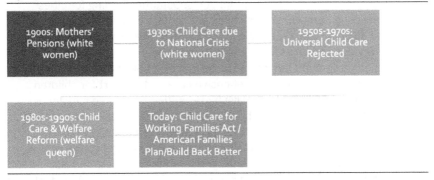

> ## Brief Journey of the Federal Policy on Child Care
>
> - 1900-1930s: During the Progressive era, women were given money to encourage them to stay at home and not use nurseries. There was a recognition that there was a need to pay women who cared for children. However, that was not enough to encourage women to stay at home. This was only available to "worthy" women who were deprived of support of a man. Black women were specifically denied because they were used to working, so did not qualify as "worthy" for these women's pensions.
> - 1930s-1940s: The Great Depression and World War II created a national child care crisis. First, the government funded emergency nursery schools to provide jobs for the unemployed, teachers, nurses, and cooks. As unemployment increased, enrollment in these emergency nurseries sharply declined. Then in World War II men were heading off to war so women were needed to work in factories. When the female workforce peaked in the early 1940s, Congress allocated more than $6 million dollars toward child care facilities for these working mothers (mostly white women). Funding was pulled after the war waned (Michel, 2012).
> - 1950s-1970s: After World War II, many white women entered the workforce (Black women had always worked), so they needed child care. To encourage mostly low-income women to work, the federal government started to look at child care program support. There was also a growing understanding about the importance of high-quality care to the healthy development of children.
> - In 1971, the United States nearly achieved a universal child care system: Congress passed the Comprehensive Child Development

Act, which would have authorized substantial funding for cities to set up comprehensive child care centers that would be open to all on a sliding fee scale and provide nutrition and medical services as well as high quality care for young children. This plan may sound familiar because it is Head Start that provided multigenerational, comprehensive care and support for children and families. We would have had a unified integrated early care and education system about 50 years ago! This legislation stated that child care was a right for all children, regardless of family income. However, due to antifeminist backlash and conservatives' desire to maintain traditional, gendered family roles, and also the fear of integration and supports for Black families, President Nixon vetoed this bill.

- 1980s–1990s. As women continued to join the workforce—married women along with higher numbers of divorced and single women heads of households—another child care movement started. In 1990, Congress established the Child Care and Development Block Grant (CCDBG). The CCDBG was focused on direct assistance to low-income families and improved supply and quality of child care. At the same time, politicians needed to ensure that the "lazy mother on public assistance who deliberately breeds children at the expense of taxpayers to fatten her monthly check," the "welfare queen," would not receive benefits. Belief in the mass existence of this near-mythical creature resulted in job requirements and tight restrictions on who qualified for benefits. We continue to see pushback on federal funds going to low-income women or paying a fair wage when this support is viewed through the prism of anti-Blackness. Jobs where Black women predominate were restricted to ensure Black women were not becoming wealthy from "just babysitting" or making babies. Thus, it is unsurprising that there is a lot of required paperwork for the early childhood provider where the compensation hardly seems to merit the amount of monitoring.

- 2000s–2020s: During the 117th Congress (2021–2022), the Child Care for Working Families Act (S. 1360) was introduced. This bill provides funds for low- to moderate-income families, including supports to infants, toddlers, and children with disabilities. The Biden Administration's American Families Plan sought to provide free, high-quality, accessible, and inclusive preschool to all three- and four-year-olds. As part of this plan, tuition-free community college and teacher scholarships would have been available

> to support ECE professionals who wanted a bachelor's degree
> or another credential that supports their work as an educator
> (The White House, 2021b). ECE professionals would also have
> received job-embedded coaching, professional development, and
> wages that reflect the importance of their work. All employees in
> participating pre-K programs and Head Start would earn at least
> $15 per hour, and those with comparable qualifications will receive
> compensation commensurate with that of kindergarten teachers.
> This plan was subsumed into the Build Back Better framework.

Let's be clear. It is a historical fact that Black and brown women were the pioneers of early childhood education and our workforce here in America. Racism and sexism against these Black and brown women led to a foundational framework that devalues early childhood education as a profession and poorly compensates its workforce. Systemic racism continues today as we spotlight the inequitable gaps in wages and leadership positions between Black early childhood professionals and their white peers. Addressing the racist and sexist foundation in the ECE sector is necessary to ensure CRABAR is realized.

One avenue being used to address the varying compensation and protection for the ECE workforce is creating a unifying framework about the ECE workforce regardless of setting and funder. There are three primary entities that have provided a professional standards framework used nationally for early childhood professionals: National Head Start; National Association for the Education of Young Children (NAEYC) and the Council for Professional Recognition (CDA). The Head Start program has staff qualifications and competency requirements based on their role (e.g., teacher, assistant teacher, home visitor, family service staff) and setting (i.e., center, home) (Office of Head Start, n.d.). Known as The Head Start Program Performance Standards (HSPPS), these professional standards help to govern Head Start programs to ensure early childhood professionals are providing high-quality, comprehensive services that support school readiness. HSPPS provides guidance to Head Start professionals and programs in areas of program governance, program operation, program structure, family and community engagement, training and technical assistance, and so forth (Head Start Early Childhood Learning and Knowledge Center, n.d.).

NAEYC (2019) has professional standards and competencies to guide ECE professionals at different levels focused on six different standards (discussed in detail later in this chapter). The Council for Professional Recognition administers the Child Development Associate (CDA), which is the only nationally recognized credentialing program for ECE professionals in the United States.

The CDA (Washington, 2019) currently has six competency standards that ECE professionals should be able to implement:

- Standard I: ensure children are physically safe and healthy and their environment is designed to promote their learning
- Standard II: understand the various domains of child development across the age range—physical development, cognitive development, communication and literacy, and creativity (e.g., dance, music, dramatic art, and visual art)
- Standard III: understand children's socio-emotional development and use positive guidance to promote positive behavior and minimize challenging behaviors
- Standard IV: know how to partner, engage, and communicate with families to support children's learning in the program and at home
- Standard V: use observation to document and plan for children's learning
- Standard VI: be a professional at all times through reflective activities, ethical approach to teaching and caring for children, and advocating for children and families

While the CDA is recognized as a comprehensive credential for ECE educators and accessible to diverse ECE professionals, its uptake and value in many programs, such as Head Start and state pre-K programs, varies, with many programs still requiring, at minimum, a bachelor's degree to be considered an ECE educator worthy of livable wage and benefits.

Power to the Profession (P2P)

As a way to address the fragmented ECE system professionals navigate through, the Power to the Profession (P2P), a national collaborative of ECE organizations, was established in 2017. The P2P initiative was established by 15 national organizations:

- American Federation of State, County and Municipal Employees
- American Federation of Teachers
- Associate Degree Early Childhood Teacher Educators
- Child Care Aware of America
- Council for Professional Recognition
- Division for Early Childhood of the Council for Exceptional Children
- Early Care and Education Consortium
- National Association for the Education of Young Children
- National Association for Family Child Care
- National Association of Early Childhood Teacher Educators

- National Association of Elementary School Principals
- National Education Association
- National Head Start Association
- Service Employees International Union
- ZERO TO THREE

P2P also included 38 partnering agencies, including the American Indian College Fund, BUILD, Center for American Progress, Center for the Study of Child Care Employment, Council of Chief State School Officers, the National Black Child Development Institute, National Women's Law Center, Trust for Learning, Montessori Accreditation Council for Teacher Education, and UnidosUS.

Through eight decision cycles, a unifying framework for the ECE professional was established, including expectations and compensation for the ECE profession, and resources, structures, and supports to advance the ECE profession. The Power to the Profession unifying framework offers recommendations in four key areas:

- Clearly defined profession with distinct responsibilities and roles
- Aligned professional licensure, pathways and preparation
- Professional Compensation
- Shared accountability and supportive infrastructure that advances the profession

(Walker, 2020)

The Power to Profession unifying framework serves as a guide within the field of early childhood aimed at strengthen the professionalization of our field. As discussed previously, early childhood historically and currently has not been publicly revered and accepted as a professional career. The P2P framework provides a unified vison, application and language within early childhood that systems and policy leaders can use. For example, when considering the P2P area of a clearly defined profession, the P2P framework creates a division of the workforce into three distinct bands: Early Childhood Educator (ECE) I, Early Childhood Educator (ECE) II, and Early Childhood Educator (ECE) III. "Each designation has an associated scope of practice, expected level of professional preparation, and expected level of mastery of the Professional Standards and Competencies for Early Childhood Educators" (Power to the Profession, 2020, p. 1). These designations have different degree expectation and classroom responsibilities. Table 5.1 provides an overview of the degree and competency levels.

As these competency levels are applied within the early childhood workforce, states then link these competency levels to workforce compensation. For example, in the state of Georgia there is a Universal PreK program which utilizes the ECE designation categories and compensates early childhood professionals accordingly. ECE teachers who are working within a Georgia PreK classroom with less than 1 year of experience with an ECE III designation makes an annual salary of $32,315 ($40,820 with certification) compared to an annual salary of $26,449 of a colleague working in a PreK classroom with an ECE II (Department of Early Care and Learning, 2022, https://www.decal.ga.gov/documents/attachments/2023TeacherSchedule.

While Table 5.1 details the ECE designations and is intended to differentiate the levels of degree and competency of early childhood professionals, the P2P framework also provides a unifying list of professional standards that early childhood systems across the country can use. This is significant because until the P2P framework, professional standards and competencies greatly varied from state to state and program to program. There are six guiding professional standards and competencies outlined by P2P (NAEYC, 2020b),

1. Child Development and Learning in Context: understand children's development over multiple dimensions in the first eight years of life
2. Family–Teacher Partnerships and Community Connections: have a respectful and trusting relationship with families to serve children and families
3. Child Observation, Documentation, and Assessment: know about and how to use assessment in ethical and culturally grounded ways to meet the needs of children, provide support, and partner with families and other professionals on behalf of children
4. Developmentally, Culturally, and Linguistically Appropriate Teaching: recognize and use a broad array of pedagogical

Table 5.1. Degree and Competency for ECE I, II, and III

ECE Designation	Degree	Competency
ECE I	Certificate/credential (e.g., CDA)	Support children birth–age 8
ECE II	Associate degree	Lead the classroom for children birth to age 5
		Support children K–Grade 3
		Guide the practice of ECE I
ECE III	Bachelor's degree or initial master's degree	Lead the classroom for children birth to age 8
		Guide the practice of ECE I and ECE II

Source: Power To The Profession. (2020). http://powertotheprofession.org/wp-content/uploads/2020/03/Power-to-Profession-Framework-03312020-web.pdf

approaches that are relevant and support children's cultural and linguistic identities and assets; although as diversity, equity and inclusion scholars, the authors question whether equity and anti-racism are fully addressed in this standard.

5. Knowledge, Application, and Integration of Academic Discipline Content in the Early Childhood Curriculum: have knowledge about how children learn in each discipline (e.g., language, math, science), have tools to use, and be able to modify and integrate knowledge in teaching practices and creation of curriculum

6. Professionalism as an Early Childhood Educator: uphold the ECE profession through continuous and collaborative learning and reflection, as well as by being informed and involved about matters regarding the profession and ECE field.

As we await the impact of P2P at the national and local levels, the need for the unifying of the ECE workforce and system continues, especially as COVID-19 continues to exact a toll on the workforce, including employees, employers, and childcare business owners. The Center for the Study of Child Care Employment (CSCCE) at the University of California–Berkeley, one of the premier organizations studying the ECE workforce and addressing policy gaps, has identified key principles to address the inequities in the ECE workforce. These principles align with the P2P unifying framework (see Table 5.2).

In essence, the CSCCE principles and the P2P unifying framework call attention to:

- Humanizing and valuing the ECE workforce as professionals and early childhood education as a profession whose voices must be heard and respected
- Eliminating the inconsistencies that lead to the unequal treatment of the ECE workforce based on your setting and the children you care for and teach
- Creating equitable and accessible pathways to education and training that recognize the baked-in racism and sexism that still operate in many institutions from higher education to school systems
- Ensuring adequate compensation and leadership opportunities across the ECE sector to disrupt the extraction of wealth from Black and brown ECE professionals and communities
- Creating a well-funded cohesive infrastructure through public investment, resources, and supports that recognizes the contributing role of ECE in many aspects of our society

Table 5.2. Alignment between Center for the Study of Child Care Employment and P2P Unifying Framework

Center for the Study of Child Care Employment Principles for Reform	P2P Unifying Framework
Amplify educators' voices, partner on decision making Respect educators' perspectives, prioritize their partnership, and create conditions for their participation in the design and implementation of policies that impact them	**A Distinct Profession** Responsibilities are to care for and promote learning for children birth to age 8
Establish consistency, eliminate fragmentation Address inconsistency in program standards and funding that fuels the current inequitable system, reinforced by reforms that address only certain sectors of ECE	**One Profession, Three Designations** A structure with three meaningful designation with an associated scope of practice, expected level of professional preparation, and expected level of mastery
Provide opportunity, ensure access Dedicated, sufficient resources and intentional strategies are required to create equitable opportunities and conditions that allow early educators to access and successfully pursue higher education	**Aligned Professional Preparation Pathways** Primary pathways aligned to designation will prepare ECE professionals for licensure at each designation.
Ensure diversity, disrupt racial stratification Women of color are overrepresented in the lowest-paying jobs, underrepresented in leadership roles, and frequently paid unequal wages for equal work; need to intentionally disrupt racial and ethnic stratification	**Professional Compensation** As ECE professionals move across the ECE competency levels, they must be compensated comparably to those with similar qualifications, experience, and job responsibility regardless of setting or age.
Ensure sustainability, dedicate sufficient funding ECE funding must be reflective of the true cost of services and thus requires substantially increased public investment and a new ECE financing structure	**Supportive Infrastructure, Shared Accountability** Create coherent systems that include professional preparation programs, employers/owners will be accountable for providing comparable compensation and benefits, professional governance to implement the P2P framework, and government agencies will use funding, legislation, and regulation to advance recommendations in their local systems

Policies and Strategies to Support ECE Educators

CRABAR practices can't truly happen in a system that continues to extract wealth by underpaying the ECE workforce. Policies focused on supporting the workforce and centered on a CRABAR lens must also work toward eradicating racism in ECE workforce leadership and compensation structures (including considering the role of reparations). It is critical that individuals, households, and corporations do not continue to profit off stolen labor and ingenuity. The present-day devaluation of the ECE workforce—a workforce that allows parents and guardians to work and businesses to thrive while building a foundation for children's lives—is in parallel with the enslavement period, when America's wealth was created through chattel slavery, brutality against and oppression of enslaved people, and the attempted eradication of Native people.

ECE professionals and those who support and benefit from this workforce must continue to call on CRABAR policies that free the ECE profession and its workforce from vestiges of the enslavement period that undervalue, disrespect, and harm this workforce. This group should recognize:

- The ECE workforce is replete with inequities when examined by race, setting type, and job position
- Recruiting and retaining same-race teachers for Black children and other children of color delivers important benefits
- Access to teachers who speak children's home language for dual language learners is valuable
- Equitable representation of lead teachers can allow access to high compensation

Meek and colleagues (2020) call for congressional, federal agencies, and state and tribal nation's involvement to address these workforce inequities, as one of the 14 policy priorities to dismantle systemic racism in ECE (the following points selected from the report are adapted and reprinted with permission). Congress can:

- Increase funding for Child Care and Development Block Grant, including the tribal set aside, and direct states/tribes to use part of the funding to increase the value of the child care subsidy to increase workforce compensation.
- Increase funding for Head Start and direct grantees to increase workforce compensation, aligned with K–12 teachers in the community.
- Increase funding for existing teacher and education leadership scholarships, fellowships, and apprenticeship programs across the

government, and prioritize Black, Indigenous, Latine, other students of color, as well as bilingual students and students with disabilities. Increases in funding should include academic support services, allow students to receive college course credits for completing post-secondary courses during high school, and provide loan relief for students who are teaching or providing other ECE services in opportunity zones or child care deserts.

• Fund a new grant program that provides pathways for paraprofessionals and others in non-lead teacher roles, especially bilingual staff and staff of color, to attain the credentials, including higher education credentials, to become lead teachers.

Federal Agencies can:

• Require pay parity, at a minimum, with K–12 teachers, across ECE programs that receive federal funds, regardless of age group taught. Strongly encourage greater compensation for non-school-based ECE programs to ensure benefit parity, including in tribal programs.

• Require states to track, report, and develop plans to address racial and other disparities in compensation and access to other publicly funded support systems, such as coaching and professional development. Work in partnership with tribal communities to track similar information.

• Provide competitive priority in discretionary funding to states who sustainably, holistically address workforce equity, such as compensation.

• Publish guidance and provide more technical assistance in how states can use grants and contracts in the Child Care Development Funding.

States and Tribal Nations can:

• Increase the value of child care subsidies to increase fairness in compensation, including pay and benefits, for child care providers.

• Expand the use of grants and contracts to prioritize and actualize fair compensation and improved working conditions (e.g., higher pay, benefits, substitute pool, lower ratios).

• Track and develop equity centered plans and analysis that address racial disparities in compensation.

• Use tiered quality rating and improvement systems to improve work conditions and provide greater compensation to bilingual

ECE professionals and those serving historically marginalized communities.
- Create regulation to establish a common pay scale and pay parity.

In addition to strategies outlined in the racial equity report, program leaders can also:

- Respect their staff and provide a mental minute, including breaks and break space, and planning time and space.
- Promote collaboration among all staff regardless of teaching position.
- Collect and disaggregate data (e.g., compensation, role) to examine for racial, gender, age group, and setting gaps, and then address any and all gaps.
- Promote their staff and create pathways for advancement.
- Access free federal and state technical assistance, resources and supports.
- Partner with other ECE sectors such as Head Start, Child Care, Pre-K.
- Enter into shared services agreements with other programs to minimize cost and maximize compensation of and benefits to the workforce. (https://childandfamilysuccess.asu.edu/sites/default/files/2021-12/14-priorities-equity-121621.pdf)

NOW WHAT?

The CRABAR framework can't be authentically achieved in ECE without addressing the structured inequities in how the workforce is treated, paid, and protected. The racism and sexism rife in ECE that is evident in a bifurcated system that stratifies compensation and value based on race, setting, and age group taught will continue to perpetuate this stratification in its practices and standards. While we still wait for federal and local governments to provide the needed resources and supports to stabilize a system created on the labor of women, especially Black and brown women, it is critical that the foundation of the profession is addressed to ensure equity and, more importantly, human rights and human dignity.

This means that it is important that everyone, especially ECE professionals, examine how racism, sexism, classism, and ableism may impact their professional behavior, whether intentionally or unintentionally. Understanding how professions with more women and women of color may be treated differently than sectors with more men and white men is important when seeking investment, resources, and justice. We must seek to understand how history may play a role in how different positions were set up and what that may mean for equal treatment and pay.

EDUCATORS' CORNER

Reflect on how our racial history is connected to your organization/company, your job/position, or your profession.

- How would you categorize your job and why? For example, is your job category professional, managerial, clerical, sales, service, etc.? Who do you think is likely to be in each of these categories and do you see a pattern by race, gender, or language?
- How much decision-making power and autonomy do you have in your job? For example, are you able to learn new things and make choices without a lot of supervision and accountability? Is this similar to other positions in industries like yours, and if so, in what way?
- How much psychological workload do you have to deal with? For example, are you being asked to meet a lot of deadlines or manage a lot of new directives or responsibilities?
- Are salaries, benefits, job assignments, and opportunities for promotion biased against you because of your race, gender, language, or a combination of these identities? If you say, yes, why do you think that is the case?

What do your responses tell you about your organization/company, job/position, or profession? If there is evidence of institutional racism, what are some steps that can be taken?

CHAPTER 6

Using the RICHER Approach to Elevate the CRABAR Practices

> I am only a teacher. My children don't need to know these things. Ending racism *is* a big thing and I am not a politician. These things happened a long time ago. My family did not own slaves. Why are we still talking about the past? Can we move on? We elected a Black president and also a Black and Asian female vice president. I just want to go to work and not get into politics. Children are children and to bring up these topics and issues separates us and takes time away from me actually learning ways to teach children how to read or play well together. Please just let me teach.

These are just some of the things we often hear when we talk with educators, school leaders, administrators, parents, and policymakers about the impact of racism in the lives of children, and what we must do to address it. If you have gotten to this part of the book, then you have read about the history and context of attending to the **why**, the **what**, the **how**, and the **who** of CRABAR practices. Now it is time to activate our social justice minds and muscles as early education professionals who are brain builders. Social justice is the active promotion of a just society by challenging systemic and institutional racism, inequality, and oppression. Activation of our social justice mind is even more critical as we see the pushback from policymakers (e.g., governors, senators) and parents (i.e., at school board meetings) about the teaching of factual history, especially when confronting the brutal past and present of how Black people, Native people, and people with marginalized identities have been treated and are being treated in the United States. In this chapter, we provide you with guidance through our RICHER framework which stands for Reeducation, Integration, Critical consciousness, Humility, Erasing racism, and Reimagination.

Dr. Gloria Ladson-Billings, premier educational scholar, reminds all educators—formal to informal—that teaching is sociopolitical and should be done with a critical consciousness lens (Ladson-Billings, 2000). This means that whether you teach science, math, language and literacy, physical education, or anything else, or are an assistant principal, program owner, or meal service specialist, you need to be aware of how the world is structured to perpetuate inequity, to share that awareness with your children (and other adults) through all opportunities that your field and your curriculum afford, and to invite them to look for solutions in any discipline. It is critical to show them how having a curious mind can awaken us to solutions that promotes the humanity of all. This means that educators should also be aware of how unfairness and bias, as well as privilege and power, are reified in school buildings, early childhood programs, and the learning process.

Sociopolitically grounded teaching is even more important for the ECE workforce. The evidence is clear that that the first five years of life is a sensitive period of brain development (NASEM, 2019), when the foundation for children's cognition, language, physical development, emotional control, conceptualization, and self-identity are being formed.

During the first 5 years of life, children's sense of self, including their racial and cultural identity, is being formed. Words, ideas, emotions shared by adults, intentionally or otherwise, are received and processed by children. This is why it is not a surprise that by the age of three, children are beginning to show racial bias. Evidence shows that white children show a preference for white people over Black people (Newheiser & Olson, 2012), demonstrate prejudiced attitudes and discriminatory behavior toward REMs (Aboud et al., 2012), and see Black people as less human and more animalistic compared to their own racial group (Costello & Hodson, 2014). Children's everyday experiences, including in their ECE settings, shape and amplify their perspectives on themselves and others. Without attention to eliminating white supremacy ideology that leads to beliefs about the worth and value of individuals based on their skin color and other phenotype clues, ECE settings will be complicit in maintaining these dehumanizing beliefs.

You may wonder how a learning institution for young children can be trafficking in white supremacy. In order to be anti-racist, teaching at all levels of education—including the early years—must flow from a consciousness rooted in an ongoing critical examination of identity, subjectivity, and the institutional influences that continue to intersect with contemporary realities. Educators have to be aware how racism and other -isms are being communicated through the curriculum and in the interactions and expectations of children. For example, if an assessment standard indicates that children should know a particular fact or behave in a particular way, there must be an interrogation of whose knowledge is being centered and who will likely be harmed when they don't meet those expectations. Uninterrogated and uncorrected, such standards can perpetuate the sweeping educational and class inequities experienced most often by racially and marginalized groups. Moreover, in historically racist social contexts—such as in the United States—constant and formidable systems ensure that the haunting legacy of past sins in the form of chattel slavery and colonization persist as a foundational influence yet to be atoned for (Feagin, 2010). In spaces where white privilege habitually dominates and thus informs the socialization process at every turn, dislodging deeply embedded bias remains an ongoing challenge.

DEFERENCE TO WHITENESS IN ECE SETTINGS

Early childhood educators committed to social justice and anti-racism should strive to cultivate an understanding of the overt and covert ways in which whiteness operates in their daily lives and in their classrooms, so that they may recognize and name inequities as they arise. While scholars have offered various conceptualizations of whiteness, for the purposes of the present chapter, we will deploy definitions intended to expose the overarching deference to whiteness as its own social identity, endowed with racialized power and privilege (Bonilla-Silva, 2017; Frankenberg, 1993; hooks, 1992).

Building on the existing scholarship, but with a view toward unpacking other essential elements, Hill et al. (2021) identify five ideological indicators of whiteness: "colorblind racism, white ignorance, white resistance, white innocence, and racial apathy" (p. 1814). Interestingly, when examined in relation to early childhood play literature, these indicators reveal several ways in which the play curriculum and play-based settings reproduce whiteness to the benefit and advantage of White children and the exclusion of Black and racially minoritized children. It should be noted here that *colorblind racism* refers to the belief that race itself is irrelevant; the term has come to connote a "minimization of racism" (Bonilla-Silva, 2017).

In play-based classrooms where educators fail to discuss race and racism and additionally overlook the opportunity to include play centers or classroom areas that reflect students' racial identities, the standards or the norms that are the most consistently communicated—and therefore institutionalized—replicate the misguided tenet that play is "race-neutral." Bryan (2020), in his work on Black "PlayCrit" (use of critical race theory to examine racially minoritized children's play experiences) literacies, pays powerful tribute to the Black children lost to anti-Black misandry in two ways. First, he reveals how the scholarship of play is largely predicated upon research conducted with the participation of white children as subjects. Second, his research both highlights and critiques the ways that Black boys' play is often viewed as deviant or via the lens of delinquency, such that their play is often criminalized (whereas white children's play is overwhelmingly perceived as "innocent").

White innocence—a term coined by Ross (1990) as cited in Hill et al. (2021)—or more plainly, the belief that white people (including white children) do not play an active role in the existence and maintenance of racism, is further expressed in how scholars traditionally interpret children's play, particularly when a racial incident is involved. For example, one of the authors of this text often delivers presentations and professional development trainings on the topic of children and race. In fact, as part of an interactive methodology, she typically invites educators to analyze play episodes culled from the existing research. In these episodes, which often depict a white child committing a racist act against a Black child, the author has consistently found that some white educators will engage in mental gymnastics (or resort to convoluted logic) in an attempt to absolve white children of wrongdoing.

If educators' underlying principles are so rigid that they effectively refuse to see white children as capable of racist acts, what will be the outcomes for Black and racially minoritized children? Clearly, whiteness reproduces and re-centers itself as inalienable, while the pain and trauma of children of color are relegated to the sidelines of the classroom (if acknowledged at all).

Our Obligation to Eliminate Racial Discrimination

We are one of the richest countries in the world; however, the question remains whether we are rich in community and humanity. In a July 2022 report, representatives of The Leadership Conference on Civil and Human Rights and The Leadership Conference Education Fund reviewed the United States' compliance with the International Convention on the Elimination of All Forms of Racial Discrimination (CERD). In their report, *Holding the Line: Combating Racial Discrimination in a Divided America*, the authors document where the United States has fallen behind in its obligations to eliminate racial discrimination (The Leadership Conference, 2022).

The report highlighted several areas that needed urgent attention, including racial profiling and excessive use of force; racist hate speech and crime; right to vote; discrimination and segregation in housing; right to health and access to health care; immigrants; and education. The report notes criminalization of students, especially Black children and other children of color, children with disabilities, and LGBTQ+ youth, in schools with school-based law enforcement: harmful policies and practices such as corporal punishment, seclusion, suspension, and expulsion, and implicit bias ingrained in disciplinary practices used inequitably against minoritized children. The report also highlights educational fiscal inequalities, with schools with larger shares of Black, Latine, and children from low-income households receiving fewer resources and supports for children compared to schools with white children and those from higher-income households. The authors propose several ways to address these racial disparities in education, including:

- Doubling the size of the Office for Civil Rights in the U.S. Department of Education to rebuild and expand the office's ability to address racial discrimination in equal access to education, including ensuring schools eliminate racial disparities in disciplinary policies and practices.
- Enacting legislation that "provide[s] safe, healthy, and inclusive school climates, including by ending federal funding for school-based law enforcement; banning the use of seclusion, restraint, and corporal punishment; and incentivizing broad reform that decreases exclusionary discipline" (p. 17).
- Ensuring fiscal equity within school districts, students' equal access to high quality educators, and the enactment of improvement plans for schools with resource inequities.

While much of the focus on education in the report focused on K–12 schooling, the racial disparities it found also track within the early education sector, including inequities in funding, discipline, and access to qualified and well-compensated educators.

THE RICHER FRAMEWORK

To move you forward on your journey, we call on you to embrace the RICHER approach (Iruka, 2020, 2022b). The United States will be enriched by eliminating the dehumanization of people and eradicating racism and bias in all aspects of our world, including in the early education programming that builds the foundation for children's healthy development and learning. We also recognize that this work should not be on the shoulders of educators only. This work should be taken on by everyone, including policymakers, organizations, business, agencies, parents and families, and community leaders.

We present the key components of the RICHER lens that we believe will lead to becoming richer in heart, mind, and social justice. RICHER focuses on reeducation, integration, critical consciousness, humility, erasing racism, and reimagination (see Figure 6.1).

Reeducation

The first R in the RICHER framework is for *reeducation* about the true history of the United States, including the attempted eradication of the Indigenous people and the brutal enslavement and rape of Africans to be this country's economic engine. That is, we must understand that the United States as we know it started with the seizure of land through fraud

Figure 6.1. The RICHER Framework

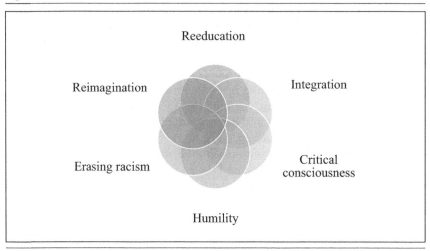

and brutality from the Native people of this continent. White people were able to claim ownership of land and force the Native people to the then-westernmost part of the United States (primarily in what is now known as the Midwest and Central Plains). On this stolen land the white conquerors created an economic engine based on chattel slavery, rape of women, and dehumanization and murder of enslaved people and their descendants.

Even after the Emancipation Proclamation, white people created a tool called racism to confer privilege and wealth on whiteness and oppression on non-white people. Racism ensures that people of color will never have access to power or privilege since all systems will be controlled by white people or whiteness as ideology (i.e., white supremacy). Part of changing one's mindset is to understand the history of oppression, brutality, inequity, classism, and most importantly, dehumanization. A critical part of being an educator is to be a historian of facts and to make visible the privilege and oppression that exist in every seat of government and are also maintained by individuals and institutions, including teachers and education leaders who often believe that children living in poverty can do only so much or should be afforded only so much opportunity.

In fact, recent studies are showing that many Americas have limited understanding of American history. For example, one study by the Zinn Education Project found that 45 of the 50 states' social studies curriculum's discussion of the Reconstruction period after the Civil War is partial or non-existent (Rosado et al., 2022). Specifically, they found that these school districts' curriculum:

- Centered white people by attending to government, politics, and policy with "little emphasis on ordinary Black people and their organizing strategies" (n.p.)
- Focused on the failures of Reconstruction policies and paid less attention to the advancements of Black people and organizers and the white supremacists who used terror and violence to dismantle any progress
- Rarely connected the dots between white supremacy and Jim Crow laws, Black Codes, and the rise of the Ku Klux Klan and in general the use of white terror to dismantle racial progress
- Did not provide a consistent definition for the Reconstruction period, instead creating comparisons between the Freedmen's Bureau and the KKK
- Limited discussion of Reconstruction and the reaction to it to the southern parts of the United States, rather than showing how racial discrimination existed throughout the Union from North and South to the West
- Failed to connect history from the Reconstruction period through to the present day and to discuss how and why the fight for racial justice is still happening and what we can learn from what worked and what did not

Let's take a moment to reflect on what we think we know about U.S. history. For many of us, it has been a long time since we studied history and it may not seem to matter in our everyday job. After all, it's the past, right? However, it does matter if we are seeking to make change in our communities, organizations, and society. The past still haunts and hurts us. For those who love history and what it tells us about the past, present and future, how are you activating that in your everyday space?

REFLECTION ACTIVITY

Reflect on the questions below about your knowledge, attitudes, and practices regarding U.S. history and its integration into your classroom and program.

- From a rating of 1 (not much) to 5 (a lot), how much do you know about U.S. history? If your rating is between 1 and 3, how can you go about changing that? What resources can you call on? If your rating is 4 to 5, how are you sharing that knowledge with colleagues, family, friends, and children?

- From a rating of 1 (very uncomfortable) to 5 (very comfortable), how comfortable do you feel teaching about history to your students? If your rating is between 1 and 3, how can you go about changing that? What resources and supports do you need to increase your efficacy and comfort level? If your rating is 4 to 5, what factors led to your comfort level on this topic and how can this be systematized to help other educators?
- In what ways do you/can you present factual U.S. history in your classroom (e.g., books, storytellers, museum visits)?
- What resources and supports do you need to present factual U.S. history in your classroom?

Integration

The I in the RICHER framework stands for the *integration* of people, communities, and especially learning spaces. The landmark 1954 Supreme Court case, *Brown v. Board of Education of Topeka*, required the provision of public education to all children on equal terms, outlawing the racial segregation of children in public schools. The idea of separate-but-equal was no longer allowed under the rule of law and Black children were to be provided equal access to education. While it took a while for all public schools to follow this law (e.g., many Southern school districts shuttered schools and terrorized Black students outside and within the school walls who attempted to desegregate schools), some level of desegregation happened.

With the sunsetting of many public school desegregation orders, schools are rapidly resegregating (McNeal, 2009; Orfield & Jarvie, 2020). The number of Black students attending racially isolated schools (i.e., non-white population of 90–100%) has increased. In the 1980s, about 33% of Black students attended segregated schools, but in 2018, this percentage rose to 40% (Orfield & Jarvie, 2020). A solution should not be on the moving of bodies—i.e., Black children being bused to white communities—but on the integration of learning resources, supports, workforce, pedagogy, curriculum, assessment, and family engagement.

Racial marginalization is apparent in how the contributions of Black, Native, Latine, and Asian people and communities are relegated to specific months (e.g., Black History Month in February, Hispanic Heritage Month in September). The contributions of communities of color to the cultural and economic fabric of the United States should be explicitly integrated into studies of history. For example, when teachers discuss how plants grow, they could talk about the indigenous practices of Native and Black communities and how they impacted national agriculture knowledge and business.

However, this level of integration cannot occur without attention to workforce, resources, and pedagogy.

Evidence shows that Black and Hispanic teachers rarely teach in white-majority schools, while white teachers make up over 40% of the workforce in public schools that are 90% or more racial minorities (Schaeffer, 2021) (see Figure 6.2). This practice limits white school leaders', teachers', and children's interactions and relationships with Black educators and knowledge givers.

Thus, beyond the integration of resources to ensure that Black and brown children get equal access to economic resources and supports, there

Figure 6.2. Percentage of U.S. Public School Teachers by Racial/Ethnic Category per School Type, School Year 2017–2018

Black, Hispanic teachers tend to work in different school environments than their White counterparts

% of U.S. public school teachers who work in each type of school who are ____, based on the 2017-18 school year

SCHOOL CLASSIFICATION	Black	Hispanic	Asian	Pacific Islander	American Indian or Alaska Native	Two or more races	White
Traditional public	6.5	9.0	2.1	0.2	0.5	1.7	80.0
Charter school	10.4	15.6	3.0	0.4	0.4	2.3	68.0
PERCENT OF MINORITY STUDENTS IN SCHOOL							
<10	0.2	1.3	0.4		0.2	0.6	97.4
10-24	1.0	2.1	0.6	0.2	0.3	1.0	94.9
25-49	2.8	4.3	1.3	0.1	0.4	1.5	89.6
50-74	6.8	8.8	2.1		0.6	2.5	79.2
75-89	10.8	14.4	3.8	0.4	0.5	2.6	67.5
90+	20.3	27.7	5.2	0.7	0.9	2.5	42.7
SCHOOL LOCALE							
City	11.8	14.0	3.1	0.2	0.3	2.1	68.5
Suburban	5.5	9.8	2.7	0.3	0.3	1.8	79.6
Town	3.7	5.8	0.9	0.3	0.9	1.7	86.8
Rural	3.6	3.8	0.5	0.1	1.0	1.3	89.7
PERCENT OF STUDENTS ELIGIBLE FOR FREE OR REDUCED-PRICE LUNCH							
0-25	1.9	4.2	2.2	0.2	0.4	1.3	89.8
26-50	3.3	5.9	1.5	0.2	0.2	1.5	87.4
51-75	6.1	8.1	1.9	0.3	0.4	2.0	81.1
76-100	13.7	17.0	2.9	0.3	0.9	2.1	63.1

Note: Data is based on a head count of full-time and part-time teachers rather than on the number of full-time-equivalent teachers reported in other tables. Detail may not sum to totals because of rounding and cell suppression. Race categories exclude persons of Hispanic ethnicity.
Source: U.S. Department of Education, National Center for Education Statistics, National Teacher and Principal Survey (NTPS).

PEW RESEARCH CENTER

Source: From Schaeffer (2021).

is a need to integrate the curriculum and pedagogical approaches. At this time, there is limited attention to culturally responsive practices, and more specifically African-centered and Indigenous-focused pedagogical practices (see textbox about African-centered teaching education).

WHAT IS AFRICAN-CENTERED EDUCATION?

African-centered education includes the following: "Identity—the importance of identifying the Black child as an African; pan-Africanism—the idea that all Black people in the world are Africans; African culture—the long-standing tradition of Blacks using African culture and language to sustain themselves and bring order to their lives and communities; African values adoption and transmission—the inclusion of an African ethos into educational process for Black children; and Black nationalism—the idea that Blacks, regardless of their specific location, constitute a nation" (E. Shockley, 2011, p. 1032). African-centered education allows children to be centered in their cultural information, resulting in them being better, more disciplined students with greater motivation for schoolwork (Asante, 1991).

African-centered teaching practices gained popularity in the 1980s and expanded rapidly in the 1990s. However, by the mid-1990s, African-centered teaching practices "came under fire in the US. Critics claimed it 'disunited America' and presented pseudo-history to students" (K. G. Shockley, 2009, p. 163), assuming it meant Black-only schools. However, African-centered education's underlying premise is to support Black children's holistic development, not compared to white children and other children, but on their own terms. Thoughtful and respectful, such teaching "inevitably tracks them towards excellence in character, spirit, and intellect" (Durden, 2007, p. 24).

Attention to integration means that educators should ensure that there is equitable access to resources for children. Educators should also make sure they are demanding more supports to help them engage in culturally responsive and sustaining practices that are indigenously bound. That is, if educators are teaching in majority Black communities, they should ensure they have training and supports on African-centered teaching similar to supports provided to programs serving high numbers of Hispanic, Asian, and other ethnic minority communities. This can only be done through the true integration of training—preservice and inservice—of different pedagogical approaches to ensure there is meaningful learning in humanizing ways for children.

Critical Consciousness

The C in the RICHER framework stands for *critical consciousness*. Paulo Freire, a Brazilian educator and philosopher, discussed the importance of ensuring that individuals had a critical consciousness lens that entails: (1) the historical, political, and social implications of a situation (i.e., the context); (2) his or her own social location in the context; (3) the intersectionality of his or her multiple identities (e.g., race, socioeconomic class, gender, sexual orientation); and (4) the inherent tensions that exist between a vision of social justice and the current societal conditions for all people (Freire, 1973). Freire believed that if people were to become critically conscious, escaping a naïve consciousness and increasing their capacity to reject the prescriptions of others, progress could be made toward dismantling systems of oppression and inequities. Similarly, Ladson-Billings (1995b) notes that students need to go beyond being "good" students and excelling academically to develop a consciousness about how cultural norms, values, traditions, and institutions reproduce inequality as well as privilege and power.

Critical consciousness is beneficial for children's development throughout the K–12 years. Studies indicate that students with higher levels of critical consciousness are more likely to have better social–emotional and academic outcomes (El-Amin et al., 2017; Heberle et al., 2020). Children with critical consciousness recognize the ways school practices might unfairly target Black students' cultural backgrounds, exclude Black youth and families from the schooling environment and learning process, and perpetuate racial inequities. For instance, students with higher critical consciousness recognize that the Black/white disparities in school suspensions might relate to the ways discipline practices are applied differently to Black and white students. With this awareness, Black students are motivated to create sociopolitical change in their schools and local communities (Bañales et al., 2019).

While there is a dearth of literature examining critical consciousness for younger age school children (i.e., elementary school students), the racial-ethnic socialization literature indicates that when children receive messages about having positive self-worth and self-identity, balanced with messages about racial inequalities, this results in positive school grades (Bowman & Howard, 1985; Sanders, 1997), academic curiosity, and persistence (Neblett et al., 2006). Racial awareness is one aspect of social development (Jagers et al., 2018) and children begin to process their racial identity in early childhood (Iruka et al., 2020).

Gay (2013) finds that culturally responsive practices develop children's critical consciousness. Thus, early childhood educators must move beyond imparting basic academic knowledge to a practice that ensures children begin to develop a critically conscious mind. This may require bringing in lessons from parents and community members or videos and artifacts that help children think critically of root causes. For example, lessons can focus on different temperatures in different parts of the community, and discussion can focus on what is it about different neighborhoods that may create high summer temperatures and flood-prone zones (e.g., limited green space and vegetation, architecture of buildings). The early years are a sensitive period to begin to develop children's curiosity and their search for information, and to begin recognizing patterns of unfairness and their possible role in addressing unfairness. Educators must engage in their own work focused on their awareness and bias. For example, when did they become aware of their race and how has that impacted their experience of the world?

Educators must also be aware of interpersonal (e.g., bias, bigotry) versus institutional racism, and their role in maintaining or dismantling white supremacy. This requires self-inquiry and attention to how systems operate invisibly unless they are made visible. Educators can ask why funding for publicly funded early childhood programs supporting children from low-income households is based on attendance and not on allocation of seats. That is, if an early childhood provider or owner allocates a seat for a child that is paid through public funds such as subsidy, why is the payment contingent on the child attending rather than automatic? Sure, it could be to ensure that the child attends the program consistently to get the full benefit, but this restriction on payment may impact early childhood programs differently, especially when serving communities that may have more social, health, and economic challenges. For example, the cost of hiring teachers, staff, food and supplies based on expected cost versus attendance may create different cost burdens that are unequally felt. Have educators inquired why certain curricula and assessments are more prominent in publicly funded programs than others, or asked about the standards and measures used to gauge quality? This is not to suggest that everything in the early childhood sector is inequitable; however, educators must be able to interrogate their own profession and environment with a critical consciousness lens to be able to translate that for young children.

Let's pause to see how critical consciousness can be activated in the classroom. These moments can be big or small, but the point is to take the time to think and talk through a situation or a question.

EDUCATORS' CORNER

A 4-year child, Shanelle, asks you during book reading time why all of the homeless people she sees when driving to school look "brown like me."

- What is your reaction to this question? Do you immediately address it or say you will discuss it later? Why or why not? Have you noticed this pattern and what was your thought? Are there similar things you have seen and thought about?

- This is a fair question from a young child who sees a pattern that concerns her. What can you do to push this query further to help students examine data, talk with community people to explore systemic inequities in their community, and develop ways to solve them as needed?
- How can you help other children to have this consciousness in their community or even in the classroom? Are some children not being treated fairly by others, children or adults?

Humility

The H in the RICHER framework stands for *humility*. Early education is usually the first experience children will have outside their home and thus it is critical that a tone is set to ensure that children feel seen, heard, and connected to their teachers, peers, and school community. Educators should examine the extent to which there is cultural concordance between children's home culture and interactions and their ECE environment. That is, there may be differences in children's freedom of movement, language usage (formal/informal), books and learning materials, and physical closeness, to name a few. Starting child care or school may be an especially jarring experience for children whose culture is different from traditional school culture. Thus, educators must recognize their lack of knowledge in recognizing a difference in children's culture from their own or the culture of the educational space.

Readers may wonder how humility can best be brought to bear as a professional advantage in terms of early childhood education. At a symbolic level, humility signifies an awareness or acceptance of subjective performance limitations pertaining to either experience with or knowledge of a topic (and a desire to engage in self-improvement). Humility seeks neither recognition nor reward; humility gives generously rather than taking and embodies the desire to serve, not lead. Further, as a contributing competency in progressive approaches to teaching and learning, humility foregrounds the experience of others by way of learning from and with collaborative groups. Humility embodies the selfless and respectful tenets of service characteristic of deep revolutionary work. More specifically, from an anti-racist perspective, racial humility is critical to disrupting white privilege in word and deed, since race-based privilege engenders a sense of entitlement (which, when allowed to run its course, may result in terror, trauma, death, and destruction for marginalized groups). By contrast, racial humility exacerbates white discomfort and emotional resistance (DiAngelo, 2016); scholars suggest that these are often impediments both to learning about race and racism and to implementing anti-racist pedagogy (Applebaum, 2017; Jayakumar & Adamian, 2017).

Cultural humility ensures educators know and understand they are the ones with privilege and power due to their knowledge and control of everything about the learning space (the schedule, curriculum assessment, behavioral expectations, and environment). As noted by Tervalon and Murray-Garcia (1998), especially in the context of race, ethnicity, class, linguistic capability, and sexual orientation, "[Early educators] must be taught to repeatedly identify and remedy the inappropriate exploitation of this power imbalance in the establishment of treatment priorities and [education] promotion activities" (p. 120). Cultural humility is a process where individuals (a) continually engage in self-reflection and self-critique as life-long learners and reflective professionals, (b) check the power imbalances in the dynamics of educator–child or educator–parent communication by using child- or parent-focused care, and (c) develop and maintain mutually respectful relationships and advocate for others (Tervalon & Murray-Garcia, 1998).

There are many ways to develop cultural humility, including recognizing how a person's belief in the superiority of their own culture shapes how they interact with children and others whose culture many be different; understanding the broader context of society; and using strategies of cultural competence. As an example, Lund and Lee (2015) engaged in a community-initiated service-learning project (SLP) within a teacher education program that raises awareness about power and privilege and countering deficit model framing. Teachers engaged in a variety of programs such as afterschool/life-skills programs, tutoring programs, mentoring programs, recreation programs, child-minding programs, family literacy programs, and programs offered by public schools. The authors found that the SLPs (Lund & Lee, 2015):

- Enhanced teachers' ability to self-reflect critically and to identify and appreciate the strengths of children and families. For example, rather than focusing on the economic and language differences of immigrant families, teachers were able to see that multilingualism was a strength and an important aspect of society, and also to move beyond their generalizations about racial and ethnic groups.
- Fostered cultural humility and greater self-awareness through building positive relationships with children of diverse backgrounds by recognizing how their own race (i.e., white) gives them power and privilege in many spaces and places. For example, one teacher noted that she was being asked for directions

and answers rather than the real leader because there was an assumption that as a white person, she was the leader of the organization. Furthermore, teachers were able to experience how to handle "uncomfortable diversity situations" that might arise in their classrooms because now they "felt a professional obligation to be able to recognize manifestations of discriminatory behavior on the part of themselves as teachers or on the part of other students." (p. 19)

Thus, professional education for cultural humility needs to anticipate and accommodate people with different motivations for being involved, such as the desire to respond appropriately to the diversity in classrooms, to address the challenges they see with this growing diversity, and their personal experience as a member of a marginalized community. Educators have unique life experiences and a range of understandings of diversity.

In another example, Brown and colleagues (2016) found that home visits to observe the sociocultural norms in homes different than their own and a community mapping activity to experience firsthand the factors that influenced their children's school experiences helped early childhood and elementary school educators to develop cultural humility. Cultural humility is a process that is ever-changing. Educators must allow themselves to be vulnerable and open to the process of learning about their own upbringing, biases, and other experiences that shape their attitudes and interactions with those who may not share their cultural backgrounds. It is also about interrogating bias and deficit frameworks that people have about groups, and seeing "problems" and "challenges" with having "others" in your learning setting rather than the humanity and assets connected with diversity and the quality and vibrancy of a diverse environment. More importantly, there is a need to see the social issues experienced by those from marginalized communities as not squarely on their shoulders. The load should be lightened by those with more privileged identities.

Erasure of Racism and Other -isms

The E in the RICHER framework stands for the *erasure* of racism in all its forms, from the systems we have created to the biases and bigotry that are a part of the root of the United States. Dismantling racism will take an "all hands on deck" approach because of the multiple levels of racism that exist. First, racism stratifies one group as valuable and worthy based on their skin color, place, gender, ability, and so much more; racism is also seen in the way that institutions like health care, education, criminal justice, and child welfare interact with individuals, families, and communities based on their identity, especially their race and ethnicity; then comes the way individuals interact with others, such as who we decide to hire, who gets a loan, who gets benefit of the doubt and who gets suspended, and who gets a warning rather than arrested during a traffic stop; and finally, the way that groups who are marginalized may begin to internalize all of the negative things said about their group (see Figure 6.3). Of critical note is the importance of understanding how historical policies have present-day impact (e.g., historic redlining policies still impact the racial wealth gap, schooling access, and mass incarceration).

There are even more aspects and effects of racism, but what is most important is that we all understand how racism is dehumanizing and negatively impacts the development, learning, and opportunities of Black children and other children of color in numerous and complex ways (Iruka, Gardner-Neblett, et al., 2022). For example, rather than seeing the word gap or achievement gap as a problem with children and their families, we must look at whose standard is being centered, whose asset is viewed as less than, whose labor was taken for free, and who has been and remains systematically excluded through racist laws and policies from opportunities, assets, and experiences (Gardner-Neblett et al., 2021). Furthermore, it is critical in dismantling racism to center the assets of families and children, such as their aspirations, diverse communication systems (e.g., Spanglish, Black English, body gestures such as nodding as greeting), their sense of family beyond blood relatives, and their spirituality.

Figure 6.3. The Different Levels of Racism and Family & Community Assets

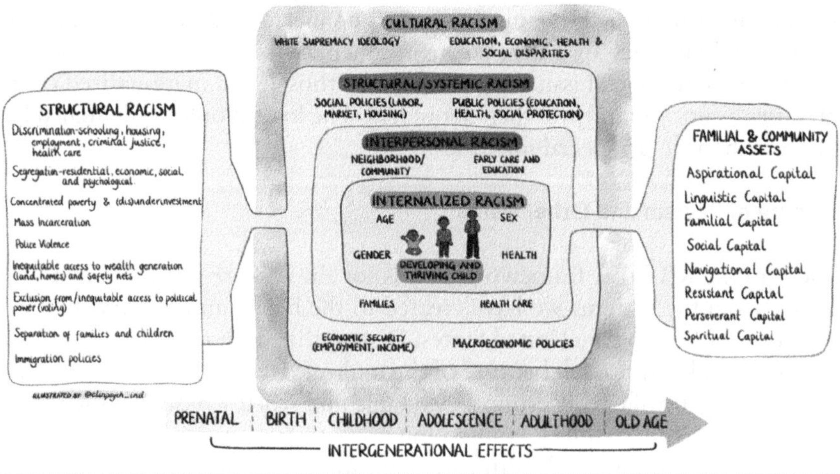

Source: Illustration by Indiana Montaque (@clinpsych_ind)

Before we continue to our next letter, let's take a moment to understand how racism and white supremacist ideology are in our DNA. In fact, some bigoted notions about who is human were embraced by some of our great and admired leaders. What if racist, sexist, or ableist language comes from those you love and admire? What does that make you think?

REFLECTION ACTIVITY

- Read the statement below and write for one minute what you think about the statement; examine how it may show up in your classroom, program, or where you live.

  "I have no purpose to introduce political and social equality between the white and the black races. There is a physical difference between the two, which, in my judgment, will probably forever forbid their living together upon the footing of perfect equality, and inasmuch as it becomes a necessity that there must be a difference, [I] am in favor of the white race having the superior position. There is a natural disgust in the minds of nearly all white people, to the idea of an indiscriminate amalgamation of the white and black race."

- What are your thoughts if I said this statement came from President Abraham Lincoln during his first debate with Stephen A. Douglas at Ottawa, Illinois, August 21, 1858? Does it hit differently that this comes from a president revered by many?

Reimagination

The last R in the RICHER framework stands for *reimagination* and radical thinking that challenges the status quo. What would it look like in your classroom or program if you reimagined that every child was able to fully access the classroom—from the materials to the conversations—in ways that confirmed their worth, value, brilliance, and humanity, and not ways that were predetermined by attitudes toward their language, skin color, economic background, or disability status? What if they were able to see themselves fully represented in community venues such as libraries, bus stops, in books and TV shows, or even in their favorite cartoon or Disney movie? We can't just wait for the next Black Panther or Encanto movie for children to celebrate the limited opportunities to see themselves in everyday matters. The system of racism has woven a story about who is worthy, valuable, and deserving of protection, promotion, and affirmation.

As an educator, what would your classroom look like if you could re-imagine it? Would you have a curriculum and assessment? If so, what would they look like and focus on? What would teaching look like if the classroom was a village and the job was to be the village that raises children thinking about their health, well-being, excellences, and most importantly their liberation and joy? That is, what would a classroom feel like when children, especially Black and brown children, can have freedom of movement, like lying on the floor during reading or standing by the window to feel the warmth of the sun, and freedom of words to combine a series of words to make a story or to mix the new words they have learned from their older sister with the words of the day? How can we reimagine the teaching enterprise to meet Ladson-Billings's call for action focused on at the minimum these three propositions: (1) Students must experience academic success; (2) students must develop and/or maintain cultural competence; and (3) students must develop a critical consciousness through which they challenge the status quo of the current social order?

Guided by Muñiz's culturally responsive reflection guide (Muñiz, 2020), we implore you to consider these eight steps to move toward CRABAR practices, starting with reflecting on one's cultural lens (see Table 6.1). Thus, getting to CRABAR practices requires introspection, such as reflecting on one's cultural lens to recognizing bias, and actions, such as bringing real world issues into the classroom and collaborating with families and communities.

NOW WHAT?

Recognize that engaging in CRABAR practices requires attention to the RICHER approach. That is, educators can improve access and opportunities for their students by building on their repertoire of *reeducation* about the history of their country and community; *integration* of their pedagogical approaches, resources, and workforce; *critical consciousness* about bias and systemic inequities; *humility* about power and privilege; *erasure of racism* and other -isms as central to teaching, and *reimagination* of what schooling (and society) can look and feel like when people's civil rights and human rights are centered.

How can you create a RICHER classroom? Are there things you can do to make this possible? For example, how much of your curriculum includes historical knowledge and activities beyond Black History and Hispanic Heritage month events? What books are on your shelves? Rather than punishing or humiliating a child, are there ways to have them see their behavior as affecting them, their peers, and their classroom culture? Are there moments in the day to give one or two kids that extra hug to let them know they matter even if the world says otherwise? How about the information you are sharing with families—rather than a report, what about a picture?

Table 6.1. Eight Competencies for Cultivating CRABAR

Competency	Questions to ask yourself	Some considerations
(1) Reflect on your own cultural lens	When did you became aware of your group membership? How does your identity shape your thinking and perceptions?	Be aware that you can unknowingly use stereotypes and microaggressions. Being culturally competent is not easy, and it is not about perfection but working through unconscious attitudes and beliefs and having humility.
(2) Recognize and redress bias in the system	Are you aware of personal and systemic bias? Are you an enabler or disrupter of systemic biases?	Culturally responsive educators understand the difference between bias at the personal and at the institutional levels and seek to understand how identity may impact equal access, opportunities, and outcomes. Asking questions and inquiring about a pattern is one way to disrupt biases.
(3) Draw on children's culture to shape curriculum and instruction	Do you look for historical accuracy and limit stereotypes? Do you incorporate children's traditions and background?	Cultural scaffolding—using a child's culture to bridge to lesson—is one strategy of culturally responsive teaching. Evaluate the curriculum and materials to ensure they are culturally responsive and representative of children, families, and communities.
(4) Bring real world issues into the classroom	Does your instruction and curriculum help children solve problems in their lives—small or big? Do you connect the curriculum, activities, or interactions to racism or issues of fairness or justice?	Consider how the classroom environment and curriculum is connected to children's lives. It could be that they went to the zoo or their favorite movie is *Encanto, Turning Red*, or *Little Mermaid*. Ask kids what is troubling them today that they need the class to help them solve; the best way of discussing fairness and privilege is by trying to solve a problem.

(continued)

Figure 6.1. (*continued*)

Competency	Questions to ask yourself	Some considerations
(5) Model high expectations for all children	Do you communicate high expectations to all children? Do you keep all children engaged and connected?	Be aware that many Black and brown children get a lot of messages about their lack of intellect and ability, so you must be attuned to this and always set a culture of high expectation. Do not allow children to disengage (close proximity, eye gaze, gestures); help them develop high expectations of themselves and provide rigorous curriculum and instruction.
(6) Promote respect for student differences	Do you help children develop respect, empathy, and understand for others who are different from them? Do you help children stand up against bias and unfair treatment?	Model and embody opening and acceptance of all. (Consider your body language and how your actions may be viewed as exclusionary.) Make sure children feel like they belong.
(7) Collaborate with families and local communities	Do you assess which families are involved and heard, and those who are not heard or seen? Do you know how to be part of children's community?	Assume all families are interested, so engage with them. Find out families' goals for their child and concerns they may have from prior school experiences (theirs or their children).
(8) Communicate in linguistically and culturally responsive ways	Do you notice similarities and differences between the style of communication with children and families? Are you able to reduce communication barriers and deficit views about different speaking styles?	Explore whether you have underlying assumptions about how someone speaks, including accents or their tone. Explore if you see a child's tone as adversarial or their normal communication style.

REFLECTION ACTIVITY

What one word describes how children feel when they are in a classroom that is committed to the RICHER Approach and the CRABAR Framework?
   If you are by yourself, think by yourself and write one word, and why.
   If you are in a group, then you can create a word cloud. You can use free services like Poll Everywhere (https://pollev.com/) or Mentimeter (https://www.mentimeter.com) to create your own group's word cloud. After completing your word cloud, you can print it out to remind you of what the anti-racist classroom feels like to a child.

Conclusion

There is no end to the fight for racial justice in early childhood. We hope this book has given you the courage, the vision, and the words to seek a more equitable future, and, more immediately, create an early learning environment that is culturally responsive, anti-bias, and anti-racist (CRABAR). The journey we took you on sought to open your eyes to the racism that is within our society, historically and contemporarily, but also within the walls of our early education system. Rather than just name this violent problem, we encourage you to activate habits in your sphere to begin to address these injustices through CRABAR practices. This means pausing and reflecting on your own understanding and awareness of systemic racism, interpersonal racism, and even internalized racism. We ask you to consider ways that CRABAR can be activated in the lessons you create for children, such as taking small interactions with children as teaching moments to counteract racism and bias especially about race, culture, and other identities. For example, when children make a negative note about a particular skin color or tone, that is a critical moment to stop and reflect on those sentiments with children and engage in a joyful and curious interaction.

We also showed you the power of spaces and how they communicate worth and value. There is a reason why there are Confederate statues in some daily spaces; they communicate information, ideology, and value. Similarly, early learning spaces communicate information, regardless of intent. In this book, we asked you to think about what values your learning spaces transmit and whether that is leading to the justice we seek. Our critical lens must be activated at all times if we are to make the change we want. We also need a fresh lens to see children's knowledge, skills, and talents. For too long, judgements about children's knowledge, skills, and talents have been centered on whiteness, ignoring Black and brown brilliance as not worthy. We call on educators to really reflect on whose lens we are using to judge children's worth and value. We must embrace the many assets that children bring to the learning space, especially when we recognize that those spaces sometimes make them invisible and demean them. How can we expect children to function in spaces where they are brutalized and unseen?

We recognize that responsibility for the change we seek does not lie solely on the shoulders of early educators, especially when they are viewed as "mere babysitters" in some circles and are not properly compensated and recognized for the work they do on behalf of children, families, communities, and society. This requires that we examine how the early education system, built on the backs of Black and brown women, continues to be haunted by its history—never to be talked about and holistically addressed. We can't expect to create a just system when educators are being treated unjustly. We recognize the importance of addressing the working conditions and compensation of the early care and education workforce if we are to see the transformative change that centers CRABAR practices and policies.

As we continue to address an unjust system across many sectors (labor, housing, criminal justice, education), our children deserve to be in safe and affirming spaces. This is especially critical for Black and brown children, as well as those who are marginalized because of their culture, language, ability, and income level. We can't stand on the sidelines while children, with no power, are asked to just bear with it. We call on caregivers, adults, system leaders, and all of us to not just stand on the sidelines but to truly engage in activating justice in the early years. We can't be the rich country we profess to be if we don't authentically engage in a RICHER approach that:

1. reeducates, acknowledges, and embraces our history (good, bad, and ugly)
2. integrates our resources, multiple intelligences, and talents
3. engages in critical consciousness about justice and fairness in all aspects of our society
4. has humility about the privilege and power we have and ensures we activate them to improve the lives of others
5. focuses our energy on dismantling racist systems, ideologies, and institutions that seek to minimize our personhood based on socially constructed identities
6. reimagines a future where equity is not an abstract term but an action that protects all from harm and trauma, promotes their health, wealth, and well-being, and most importantly, preserves every cultural identity, language, custom, and heritage as a critical asset for society

As you move forward with these action items and next steps, know that you hold the power to ensure racial justice in early childhood. You have tools inside and outside the classroom walls: the pedagogical approach you use, your efforts to fully see and assess children, the way you set up an anti-racist program and classroom, the resources you use to extend children's learning to how you partner with families. Just remember, WE are the change WE seek!

Resources

Brookes. (n.d.). *Early childhood anti-racism resources.* https://brookespublishing.com/early-childhood-anti-racism-resources/

Center of Excellence for Infant & Early Childhood Mental Health Consultation. (n.d.). *Equity.* https://www.iecmhc.org/resources/equity/

Children's Institute (n.d.). *Racial equity resources for early childhood.* https://childinst.org/key-topics/centering-racial-equity-in-early-childhood/

Early Childhood Technical Assistance Center (n.d.). *Racial equity.* https://ectacenter.org/topics/racialequity/

Educators for Antiracism (n.d.). *Early childhood antiracism resources.* https://www.edantiracism.com/early-childhood

Huang, C., Harris, K., & Curenton-Jolly, S. (2021). *Racially affirming books for Asian American Pacific Islander children and families.* Center on the Ecology of Early Development, Wheelock College of Education & Human Development, Boston University. https://www.bu-ceed.org/uploads/1/3/3/0/133043669/ceed__aapi_book_list_2021__1_.pdf

Iruka, I. U., Curenton, S. M., Durden, T. R., & Escayg, K.-A. (2020). *Don't look away: Embracing anti-bias classrooms.* Gryphon House.

Kaplan (n.d.). *Diversity, equity, and inclusion resources.* https://blog.kaplanco.com/tag/diversity-equity-inclusion

Kaplan (n.d.). *Classroom cultural diversity kit.* https://www.kaplanco.com/product/37251/classroom-cultural-diversity-kit?c=50%7CDE1010

NAEYC (n.d.). *Equity Resources: Living the Statement.* https://www.naeyc.org/equity/position-statement-resources

Sims, J., Curenton, S. M., & Rochester, S. (2020). *Racially affirming books for Black children.* Center on the Ecology of Early Development, Wheelock College of Education & Human Development, Boston University. https://www.bu-ceed.org/uploads/1/3/3/0/133043669/tps_booklist.pdf

References

Aboud, F. E., Tredoux, C., Tropp, L. R., Brown, C. S., Niens, U., & Noor, N. M. (2012). Interventions to reduce prejudice and enhance inclusion and respect for ethnic differences in early childhood: A systematic review. *Developmental Review*, 32(4), 307–336. https://doi.org/https://doi.org/10.1016/j.dr.2012.05.001

Addo, F. R., Houle, J. N., & Simon, D. (2016). Young, Black, and (still) in the red: Parental wealth, race, and student loan debt. *Race and Social Problems*, 8(1), 64–76. https://doi.org/https://doi.org/10.1007/s12552-016-9162-0

Adkison-Bradley, C., Terpstra, J., & Dormitorio, B. (2014). Child discipline in African American families: A study of patterns and context. *The Family Journal: Counseling and Therapy for Couples and Families*, 22, 198–205.

Allen, R., Shapland, D. L., Neitzel, J., & Iruka, I. U. (2021). Creating anti-racist early childhood spaces. *YC Young Children*, 76(2), 49–54.

Anderson, R. E., Heard-Garris, N., & DeLapp, R.C.T. (2021). Future directions for accinating children against the American endemic: Treating racism as a virus. *Journal of Clinical Child & Adolescent Psychology*, 1–16. https://doi.org/10.1080/15374416.2021.1969940

Applebaum, B. (2017). Comforting discomfort as complicity: White fragility and the pursuit of invulnerability. *Hypatia*, 32(4), 862–875. doi:10.1111/hypa.12352

Archer, E. (2017). The assessment purpose triangle: Balancing the purposes of educational assessment. *Frontiers in Education*, 2, 1–7. https://doi.org/10.3389/feduc.2017.00041

Asante, M. (1991). The Afrocentric idea in education. *The Journal of Negro Education*, 60, 170–180.

Asante-Muhammad, D., Buell, J., & Devine, J. (2021). *60% Black homeownership: A radical goal for Black wealth development*. National Community Reinvestment Coalition. https://ncrc.org/60-black-homeownership-a-radical-goal-for-black-wealth-development/

Ash, A. N., Hill, R., Risdon, S., & Jun, A. (2020). Anti-racism in higher education: A model for change. *Race and Pedagogy Journal: Teaching and Learning for Justice*, 4(3), 2.

Austin, L. J. E., Edwards, B., Chavez, R., & Whitebook, M. (2019). *Racial wage gaps in early education employment*. Center for the Study of Child Care Employment, University of California–Berkeley. https://cscce.berkeley.edu/racial-wage-gaps-in-early-education-employment/

Aydoğan, C., Farran, D. C., & Sağsöz, G. (2015). The relationship between kindergarten classroom environment and children's engagement. *European Early*

Childhood Education *Research Journal, 23*(5), 604–618. https://doi.org/10 .1080/1350293x.2015.1104036

Bacher-Hicks, A., Billings, S. B., & Deming, D. J. (2021). Proving the school-to-prison pipeline. *Education Next, 21*(4). https://www.educationnext.org/proving -school-to-prison-pipeline-stricter-middle-schools-raise-risk-of-adult-arrests/

Bagnato, S. J., Neisworth, J. T., & Pretti-Frontczak, K. (2010). LINKing authentic assessment and early childhood intervention: Best measures for best practice (2nd ed.). Paul H Brookes Publishing.

Bailey, Z. D., Krieger, N., Agénor, M., Graves, J., Linos, N., & Bassett, M. T. (2017). Structural racism and health inequities in the USA: evidence and interventions. *The Lancet, 389*(10077), 1453–1463. https://doi.org/https://doi.org/10.1016 /S0140-6736(17)30569-X

Bañales, J., Aldana, A., Richards-Schuster, K., Flanagan, C. A., Diemer, M. A., & Rowley, S. J. (2019). Youth anti-racism action: Contributions of youth perceptions of school racial messages and critical consciousness. *Journal of Community Psychology, 49*, 3079–3100. https://doi.org/10.1002/jcop.22266

Berry, D. R. (2017). *The Price for their pound of flesh: The value of the enslaved, from womb to grave, in the building of a nation.* Beacon.

Black, D. W., & Crolley, A. (2022, April 15). Legacy of Jim Crow still affects funding for public schools. *The Conversation.* https://theconversation.com/legacy-of -jim-crow-still-affects-funding-for-public-schools-181030

Blackson, E. A., Gerdes, M., Segan, E., Anokam, C., & Johnson, T. J. (2022). Racial bias toward children in the early childhood education setting. *Journal of Early Childhood Research, 20*(3), 277–292. https://doi.org/10.1177/1476718x221087051

Bobbitt, K. C., & Gershoff, E. T. (2016). Chaotic experiences and low-income children's social-emotional development. *Children and Youth Services Review, 70*, 19–29. https://doi.org/10.1016/j.childyouth.2016.09.006

Bonilla-Silva, E. (2017). *Racism without racists: Color-blind racism and the persistence of racial inequality in America.* Rowman & Littlefield.

Boutte, G., & Bryan, N. (2019). When will Black children be well? Interrupting anti-Black violence in early childhood classrooms and schools. *Contemporary Issues in Early Childhood, 22*(3), 232–243. https://doi.org/10.1177/1463949119890598

Bowman, P. J., & Howard, C. (1985). Race-related socialization, motivation, and academic achievement: A study of Black youths in three-generation families. *Journal of the American Academy of Child Psychiatry, 24*(2), 134–141.

Brandt, G. 1986). *The realization of anti-racist teaching.* Falmer Press.

Brown, E. L., Vesely, C. K., & Dallman, L. (2016). Unpacking biases: Developing cultural humility in early childhood and elementary teacher candidates. *Teacher Educators' Journal, 9*, 75–96.

Brucato, B. (2020). Policing race and racing police: The origin of US police in slave patrols. *Social Justice, 47*(3/4), 115–136. https://www.jstor.org/stable/27094596

Bryan, N. (2020). Shaking the bad boys: Troubling the criminalization of black boys' childhood play, hegemonic white masculinity and femininity, and the school playground-to-prison pipeline. *Race Ethnicity and Education, 23*(5), 673–692. https://doi.org/10.1080/13613324.2018.1512483

Burton, L. (2007). Childhood adultification in economically disadvantaged families: A conceptual model. *Family Relations, 56*(4), 329–345.

Cassidy-Bushrow, A. E., Sitarik, A. R., Havstad, S., Park, S. K., Bielak, L. F., Austin, C., Johnson, C. C., & Arora, M. (2017). Burden of higher lead exposure in African-Americans starts in utero and persists into childhood. *Environment International*, *108*, 221–227. https://doi.org/https://doi.org/10.1016/j.envint.2017.08.021

Caven, M. (2020, July 28). *Why we need an anti-racist approach to social and emotional learning*. Education Deveopment Center. https://edc.org/blog/why-we-need-anti-racist-approach-social-and-emotional-learning

Centers for Disease Control and Prevention (2019). Racial and ethnic disparities continue in pregnancy-related deaths. https://www.cdc.gov/media/releases/2019/p0905-racial-ethnic-disparities-pregnancy-deaths.html?utm_campaign=later-linkinbio-mallorie.the.midwife&utm_content=later-7624080&utm_medium=social&utm_source=instagram

Cherry, M. A., & Harrison, V. (2019). *Hair love*. Kokila.

The Children's Community School. (2018). *They're not too young to talk about race*. Author. http://www.childrenscommunityschool.org/wp-content/uploads/2018/02/theyre-not-too-young-1.pdf

Cooke, A. N., & Halberstadt, A. G. (2021). Adultification, anger bias, and adults' different perceptions of Black and White children. *Cognition and Emotion*, 1–7. https://doi.org/10.1080/02699931.2021.1950127 ve

Costello, K. and Hodson, G. (2014), Explaining dehumanization among children: The interspecies model of prejudice. *Br. J. Social Psychology*, *53*, 175–197. https://doi-org.libproxy.lib.unc.edu/10.1111/bjso.12016

Curenton, S. M., & Franco, X. (2022). *The Culturally Responsive Anti-Bias Anti-Racist (CRABAR) Curriculum Audit Tool*. Center on the Ecology of Early Development.

Curenton, S. M., & Franco, X. (2022). *Culturally Responsive Anti-Bias Anti-Racist Curriculum (CRABAR) Audit Tool for Literacy*. Center on the Ecology of Early Development, Boston University [unpublished].

Curenton, S. M., Harris, K., Rochester, S. E., Sims, J., & Ibekwe-Okafor, N. (2022). Promoting racial literacy in early childhood: Storybooks and conversations with young black children. *Child Development Perspectives*, *16*(1), 3–9.

Curenton, S. M., & Iruka, I. U. (2013). *Cultural competence in early childhood education*. Bridgepoint Education.

Curenton, S. M., Iruka, I. U., Humphries, M., Jensen, B., Durden, T., Rochester, S. E., Sims, J., Whittaker, J. V., & Kinzie, M. B. (2019). Validity for the Assessing Classroom Sociocultural Equity Scale (ACSES) in early childhood classrooms. *Early Education and Development*, *31*(2), 284–303. https://doi.org/10.1080/10409289.2019.1611331

Curenton, S. M., Rochester, S. E., Sims, J., Ibekwe-Okafor, N., Iruka, I. U., García-Miranda, A. G., & Whittaker, J. (2022). Antiracism defined as equitable sociocultural interactions in prekindergarten: Classroom racial composition makes a difference. *Child Development*, *93*(3), 681–698.

Dancy, T. E., Edwards, K. T., & Earl Davis, J. (2018). Historically white universities and plantation politics: Anti-Blackness and higher education in the Black Lives Matter era. *Urban Education*, *53*(2), 176–195.

Darling-Hammond, L. (1998). *Unequal opportunity: Race and education*. Brookings. https://www.brookings.edu/articles/unequal-opportunity-race-and-education/

Davis, J., & Marsh, N. (2020). Boys to men: The cost of 'adultification' in safeguarding responses to black boys. *Critical and Radical Social Work, 8*(2), 255–259. https://doi.org/10.1332/204986020X15945756023543

Davis, K., & MacNaughton, G. (2009). Introduction: Thinking differently: The call and the desire. In G. MacNaughton & K. Davis (Eds.), *Race and early childhood education: An international approach to identity, politics, and pedagogy* (pp. 1–14). Palgrave Macmillan.

de Brey, C., Musu, L., McFarland, J., Wilkinson-Flicker, S., Diliberti, M., Zhang, A., Branstetter, C., & Wang, X. (2019). *Status and Trends in the Education of Racial and Ethnic Groups 2018 (NCES 2019-038).* U.S. Department of Education, National Center for Education Statistics. https://nces.ed.gov/pubsearch/pubsinfo.asp?pubid=2019038dew.jstor.org/stable/

Dei, G. J. S. (1996). *Anti-racism education: Theory and practice.* Fernwood.

De la Luz Ibarra, M. (2000). Mexican immigrant women and the new domestic labor. *Human Organization, 59*(4), 452–464.

de la Peña, C. M., Pineda, L., & Punsky, B. (2019). Working with parents and children separated at the order: Examining the impact of the zero tolerance policy and beyond. *Journal of Child & Adolescent Trauma, 12*(2), 153–164. https://doi.org/10.1007/s40653-019-00262-4

Delpit, L. (2006). *Other people's children: Cultural conflict in the classroom.* The New Press.

Department of Early Care and Learning (2022). *2022–2023 Salary Schedule for Pre-K Lead Teachers.* Retrieved January 30, 2023 from https://www.decal.ga.gov/documents/attachments/2023TeacherSchedule.pdf.

Derman-Sparks, L. (1989). *Anti-bias curriculum: Tools for empowering young children.* National Association for the Education of Young Children.

Derman-Sparks, L., Edwards, J. O. & Goins, C. (2020). *Anti-bias education for young children and ourselves* (2nd ed.). National Association for the Education of Young Children.

DiAngelo, R. (2016). WHITE FRAGILITY. *Counterpoints, 497*, 245–253. http://www.jstor.org/stable/45157307

Dobbins, D., McCready, M., & Rackas, L. (2016). *Unequal access: Barriers to early childhood education for boys of color.* Child Care Aware. https://www.childcareaware.org/wp-content/uploads/2016/10/UnequalAccess_BoysOfColor.pdf

Dörnyei, Z., & Muir, C. (2019). Creating a motivating classroom environment. In X. Gao (Ed.), *Second Handbook of English Language Teaching* (pp. 719–736). https://doi.org/10.1007/978-3-030-02899-2_36

Dumas, M. J., & Ross, K. M. (2016). "Be real black for me": Imagining BlackCrit in education. *Urban Education, 51*(4), 415–442. https://doi.org/10.1177/0042085916628611

Durden, T. R. (2007). African centered schooling: Facilitating holistic excellence for Black children. *Negro Educational Review, 58*(1/2), 23–34.

Dynia, J. M., Schachter, R. E., Piasta, S. B., Justice, L. M., O'Connell, A. A., & Yeager Pelatti, C. (2018). An empirical investigation of the dimensionality of the physical literacy environment in early childhood classrooms. *Journal of Early Childhood Literacy, 18*(2), 239–263. https://doi.org/10.1177/1468798416652448

Earick, M. E. (2010). The power of play and language on early childhood racial identity in three U.S. schools. *Diaspora, Indigenous, and Minority Education, 4*(2), 131–145. https://doi.org/10.1080/15595691003635955

Early, D. M., Iruka, I. U., Ritchie, S., Barbarin, O. A., Winn, D.-M. C., Crawford, G. M., Frome, P. M., Clifford, R. M., Burchinal, M., Howes, C., Bryant, D. M., & Pianta, R. C. (2010). How do pre-kindergarteners spend their time? Gender, ethnicity, and income as predictors of experiences in pre-kindergarten classrooms. *Early Childhood Research Quarterly, 25*(2), 177–193. https://doi.org/10.1016/j.ecresq.2009.10.003

Economic Policy Institute. (2022, May). *State Unemployment by Race and Ethnicity.* https://www.epi.org/indicators/state-unemployment-race-ethnicity-2021q4-2022q1/

EdBuild. (2019). *$23 Billion.* https://edbuild.org/content/23-billion/full-report.pdf

El-Amin, A., Seider, S., Graves, D., Tamerat, J., Clark, S., Soutter, M., Johannsen, J., & Malhotra, S. (2017). Critical consciousness: A key to student achievement. *Phi Delta Kappan, 98*(5), 18–23. https://doi.org/10.1177/0031721717690360

Epstein, J. L. (2019). Theory to practice: School and family partnerships lead to school improvement and student success. In *School, family and community interaction* (pp. 39–52). Routledge.

Escayg, K-.A. (2018). The missing links: Enhancing anti-bias education with anti-racist education. *Journal of Curriculum, Teaching and Leadership in Education, 3*(1), 4, 15–20.

Escayg, K.-A. (2019). "Who's got the power?": A critical examination of the anti-bias curriculum. *International Journal of Child Care and Education Policy, 13*(6), 1–18. https://doi.org/10.1186/s40723-019-0062-9

Escayg, K.-A. (2020a). Teaching and learning guide for: Anti-racism in U.S. early childhood education: Foundational principles. *Sociology Compass, 14*(4), 1–5. https://doi.org/10.1111/soc4.12819

Escayg, K.-A. (2020b). What is whiteness? Centering the experiences and perspectives of African American children (Unpublished paper). University of Nebraska–Omaha.

Escayg, K. A. (2021). The "race" in "RECE": Reconceptualizing play-based learning through an anti-racist lens. In *Reconceptualizing Quality in Early Childhood Education, Care and Development: Understanding the Child and Community* (pp. 269–287). Springer International Publishing.

Escayg, K.-A. (2022). I love me! Positioning Black identity at the centre of play pedagogy. In K. Murray, A. Te, & J. Watt (Eds.), *My best idea: Culturally relevant pedagogy* (vol. 2., pp. 26–33). Rubicon.

Escayg, K.-A. & Farago, F. (in press). Anti-racist educators. In M. Tesar (Ed.), *The Bloomsbury Encyclopedia of Social Justice in Education.*

Essien, I. (2017). Teaching Black boys in early childhood education: Promising practices from exemplar teachers. *Journal of African American Males in Education, 8*(2), 5–21.

Etter, K., & Capizzano, J. (2022). *Knocking it all down: Why we need to build a new quality rating improvement system.* Policy Equity Group. https://policyequity.com/qris-building-the-case-for-knocking-it-down/

Fantuzzo, J., McWayne, C., Perry, M. A., & Childs, S. (2004). Multiple dimensions of family involvement and their relations to behavioral and learning competencies for urban, low-income children. *School Psychology Review, 33*(4), 467–480.

Feagin, J. (2010). *The White racial frame: Centuries of framing and counter-framing.* Routledge.

Fisher, P. (2021, July). *Who is providing for child care providers?* University of Oregon, RAPID-EC. https://static1.squarespace.com/static/5e7cf2f62c45da32f3c60 65e/t/60f979d6e6d4d36da3abebde/1626962390564/who-is-providing-for -providers.pdf

Ford, D. Y., Harris, J. J. III, Tyson, C. A., & Trotman, M. F. (2001). Beyond deficit thinking: Providing access for gifted African American students. *Roeper Review, 24*(2), 52–58.

Ford, D. Y., & Helms, J. E. (2012). Overview and introduction: Testing and assessing African Americans: "Unbiased" tests are still unfair. *The Journal of Negro Education, 81*(3), 186–189.

Ford, D. Y., & Moore, J. L. (2013). Understanding and eversing underachievement, low achievement, and achievement gaps among high-ability African American males in urban school contexts. *The Urban Review, 45*(4), 399–415. https://doi .org/10.1007/s11256-013-0256-3

Forman, S. R., Foster, J. L., & Rigby, J. G. (2022). School leaders' use of social-emotional learning to disrupt whiteness. *Educational Administration Quarterly, 58*(3), 351–385. https://doi.org/10.1177/0013161X211053609

Frankenberg, R. (1993). *White women, race matters: The social construction of whiteness.* University of Minnesota Press.

Freire, P. (1973). *Education for critical consciousness.* Seabury Press.

Friedman-Krauss, A. H., Barnett, W. S., Weisenfeld, G. G., Kasmin, R., DiCrecchio, N., & Horowitz, M. (2018). *The state of preschool 2017: State preschool yearbook.* National Institute for Early Education Research, Rutgers University.

Gardner-Neblett, N., Iruka, I. U., & Humphries, M. (2021). Dismantling the Black-White achievement gap paradigm: Why and how we need to focus instead on systemic change. *Journal of Education.* https://doi.org/10.1177/002205742110 31958

Gardner-Neblett, N., Pungello, E. P., & Iruka, I. U. (2012). Oral narrative skills: Implications for the reading development of African American children. *Child Development Perspectives, 6*(3), 218–224.

Gautier, P. A., & Zenou, Y. (2010). Car ownership and the labor market of ethnic minorities. Journal of *Urban Economics, 67*(3), 392–403. https://doi.org /https://doi.org/10.1016/j.jue.2009.11.005

Gay, G. (2000). *Culturally responsive teaching: Theory, practice and research.* Teachers College Press.

Gay, G. (2013). Culturally responsive teaching principles, practices, and effects. In H. R. Milner IV & K. Lomotey (Eds.), *Handbook of urban education* (pp. 353–372). Routledge.

Gilliam, W. S., Maupin, A. N., Reyes, C. R., Accavitti, M., & Shic, F. (2016). *Do early educators' implicit biases regarding sex and race relate to behavior expectations and recommendations of preschool expulsions and suspensions* [Research brief]. Yale University Child Study Center. https://medicine.yale.edu /childstudy/policy-and-social-innovation/zigler/publications/preschool implicit bias policy brief_final_9_26_276766_54643_v1.pdf

Goff, P. A., Jackson, M. C., Di Leone, B. A. L., Culotta, C. M., & DiTomasso, N. A. (2014). The essence of innocence: consequences of dehumanizing Black children. *Journal of Personality and Social Psychology, 106*(4), 526–545.

Guo, Y., Justice, L. M., Kaderavek, J. N., & McGinty, A. (2012). The literacy environment of preschool classrooms: Contributions to children's emergent literacy growth. *Journal of Research in Reading, 35*(3), 308-327. https://doi.org/10 .1111/j.1467-9817.2010.01467.x

Hale, J. E. (2001). *Learning while Black: Creating educational excellence for African American children*. JHU Press.

Halle, T. G., & Darling-Churchill, K. E. (2016). Review of measures of social and emotional development. *Journal of Applied Developmental Psychology, 45*, 8–18. https://doi.org/10.1016/j.appdev.2016.02.003

Hamily, D. (2022). Black joy in white spaces: Maintaining the radical power of resistance. *AJE Forum*. https://www.ajeforum.com/black-joy-in-white-spaces-main taining-the-radical-power-of-resistance-by-dwayne-hamilton-jr/

Hamre, B. K., & Pianta, R. C. (2007). Learning opportunities in preschool and early elementary classrooms. In R. C. Pianta, M. J. Cox, & K. L. Snow (Eds.), *School readiness and the transition to kindergarten in the era of accountability* (pp. 49–83). Paul H. Brookes Publishing.

Harms, T., Clifford, R. M., & Cryer, D. (1998). *Early childhood environment rating scale* (Revised ed.). Teachers College Press.

Hazelbaker, T., Brown, C. S., Nenadal, L., & Mistry, R. S. (2022). Fostering anti-racism in white children and youth: Development within contexts. *American Psychologist, 77*(4), 497–509. https://doi.org/10.1037/amp0000948

Head Start Early Childhood Learning and Knowledge Center (n.d.) Retrieved January 30, 2023 from https://eclkc.ohs.acf.hhs.gov/policy/45-cfr-chap-xiii/1302-92 -training-professional-development.

Heath, S. B. (1989). Oral and literate traditions among Black Americans living in poverty. *American Psychologist, 44*(2), 367–373. https://doi.org/10.1037/0003 -066X.44.2.367 —

Heberle, A. E., Rapa, L. J., & Farago, F. (2020). Critical consciousness in children and adolescents: A systematic review, critical assessment, and recommendations for future research. *Psychological Bulletin, 146*(6), 525–551. https://doi.org/10 .1037/bul0000230

Hill, L., Artiga, S., & Ranji, U. (2022). Racial Disparities in Maternal and Infant Health: Current Status and Efforts to Address Them. *Kaiser Family Foundation*. https://www.kff.org/report-section/racial-disparities-in-maternal-and-infant -health-an-overview-issue-brief/

Hill, T., Mannheimer, A., & Roos, J. M. (2021). Measuring White Fragility. *Social Science Quarterly, 102*(4), 1812–1829. https://doi.org/10.1111/ssqu.12985

Hilliard, A. G. (1997). Language, culture and the assessment of African American children. In A. L. Goodwin (Ed.), *Assessment for equity and inclusion: Embracing all our children* (pp. 229–240). Routledge.

Hilliard, A. G. (2003). No mystery: Closing the achievement gap between Africans and excellence. In T. Perry, C. Steele, & A. G. Hilliard, *Young, gifted, and Black: Promoting high achievement among African American students* (pp. 131–165). Beacon Press.

Hoffman, K. M., Trawalter, S., Axt, J. R., & Oliver, M. N. (2016). Racial bias in pain assessment and treatment recommendations, and false beliefs about biological differences between blacks and whites. *Proceedings of the National Academy of Sciences, 113*(16), 4296–4301. https://doi.org/10.1073/pnas.1516047113

hooks, b. (1992). Representing whiteness in the black imagination In *Black looks: Race and representation* (pp. 338–346). Routledge.

Hughes, D., Rodriguez, J., Smith, E. P., Johnson, D. J., Stevenson, H. C., & Spicer, P. (2006). Parents' ethnic-racial socialization practices: A review of research and directions for future study. *Developmental Psychology, 42*(5), 747–770. https://doi.org/10.1037/0012-1649.42.5.747

Hughes, M., Kiecolt, K. J., Keith, V. M., & Demo, D. H. (2015). Racial identity and well-being among African Americans. *Social Psychology Quarterly, 78*(1), 25–48.

Husband, T., & Escayg, K. A. (2022). "Safe and Sound": Anti-racist curriculum models for the early years classroom. *Mid-Western Educational Researcher, 34*(2), 168–182.

Hussar, B., Zhang, J., Hein, S., Wang, K., Roberts, A., Cui, J., Smith, M., Bullock Mann, F., Barmer, A., & Dilig, R. (2020). *The condition of education 2020* (NCES 2020-144). National Center for Education Statistics. https://nces.ed.gov/pubs2020/2020144.pdf

Iruka, I. U. (2020, August 6). *Embracing anti-racist approaches and centering race and racism in the Life Course research agenda.* Presentation at Life Course Intervention Research Network Meeting.

Iruka, I. U. (2022a). *Strengthening family and community partnership and engagement: Using a culturally responsive, anti-bias lens.* Children's Equity Project and Vermont Child Development Division. https://vermontkidsdata.org/wp-content/uploads/2021/04/Strengthening-Family-and-Community-Partnership-and-Engagement.pdf

Iruka, I. U. (2022b). From a pedagogy of poverty to a RICHER framework. In M. Sykes and K. Ostendorf (Eds.), *Child care justice: Transforming the system of care for young children* (pp. 70–86). Teachers College Press.

Iruka, I. U., Curenton, S. M., Durden, T. R., & Escayg, K. A. (2020). *Don't look away: Embracing anti-bias classrooms.* Gryphon House.

Iruka, I., Curenton, S., & Eke, W. (2014). *The CRAF-E4 Family Engagement Model: Building practitioners' competence to work with diverse families.* Academic Press.

Iruka, I. U., Forte, A., Curenton, S., & Sims, J. (2022a). *Family Cultural Wealth Survey.* Unpublished Instrument. RISER Network: The University of North Carolina at Chapel Hill and Boston University.

Iruka, I. U., Gardner-Neblett, N., Telfer, N. A., Ibekwe-Okafor, N., Curenton, S. M., Sims, J., Sansbury, A. B., & Neblett, E. W. (2022b). Effects of racism on child development: Advancing antiracist developmental science. *Annual Review of Developmental Psychology, 4*, 109–132. https://doi.org/10.1146/annurev-devpsych-121020-031339

Iruka, I. U., & Hawkins, C. (2022). Making the unique experiences of young black girls visible. In R. Mayes, M. Shavers and J. L. Moore, II (Eds.), *African American female students in preK–12 schools and beyond: Informing research, policy, and practice* (pp. 7–27). Emerald Publishing Limited.

Iruka, I. U., Jones Harden, B. P., Bingham, G., Esteraich, J., & Green, S. (2018). Profiles of parenting for low-income families and links to children's preschool outcomes. *Early Education and Development, 29*(4), 515–539. https://doi.org /10.1080/10409289.2018.1440843

Jacobs, M. D. (2008). The Great White Mother: Maternalism and American Indian child removal in the American West, 1880–1940. In E. Jameson & S. McManus (Eds.), *One step over the line: Toward a history of women in the North American West* (pp. 191–213). University of Alberta Press. https://digitalcommons .unl.edu/historyfacpub/106

Jagers, R. J., Rivas-Drake, D., & Borowski, T. (2018, November). *Equity & social and emotional learning: A cultural analysis* [Brief]. Measuring SEL Frameworks Briefs, Collaborative for Academic, Social, and Emotional Learning. https:// measuringsel.casel.org/wp-content/uploads/2018/11/Frameworks-Equity.pdf

Jagers, R. J., Rivas-Drake, D., & Williams, B. (2019). Transformative social and emotional learning (SEL): Toward SEL in service of educational equity and excellence. *Educational Psychologist, 54*(3), 162–184. https://doi.org/10.1080 /00461520.2019.1623032

Jang, C., & Lee, H. (2022). A review of racial disparities in infant mortality in the US. *Children, 9*(2), 257. doi: http://dx.doi.org/10.3390/children9020257

Jayakumar, U. M., & Adamian, A. S. (2017). The fifth frame of colorblind ideology: Maintaining the comforts of colorblindness in the context of white fragility. *Sociological Perspectives, 60*(5), 912–936. https://www.jstor.org/stable/26579842

Jones, C. P. (2000). Levels of racism: a theoretic framework and a gardener's tale. *American Journal of Public Health, 90*(8), 1212–1215. https://doi.org/10.2105 /ajph.90.8.1212

Jones, J. M. (1972). *Prejudice and racism.* Addison Wesley.

Katznelson, I., & Mettler, S. (2008). On race and policy history: A dialogue about the G.I. Bill. *Perspectives on Politics, 6*(3), 519–537. https://www.jstor.org /stable/20446759

Kids Count Data Center. (2018, April 13). Black children continue to be disproportionately represented in foster care. https://datacenter.kidscount.org/updates /show/264-us-foster-care-population-by-race-and-ethnicity

King, M. L., Jr. (1968). *Where do we go from here: Chaos or community?* Beacon Press.

King, S. (2020). From African American vernacular English to African American language: Rethinking the study of race and language in African Americans' speech. *Annual Review of Linguistics, 6*, 285–300.

King, T. (2003). *The truth about stories: A native narrative.* House of Anansi.

Kinkead-Clark, Z., & Escayg, K.-A. (2021). Preface. In Z. Kinkead-Clark & K.-A. Escayg (Eds), *Reconceptualizing quality in early childhood education, care and development: Understanding the child and community* (pp. v–xiv). Palgrave Macmillan.

Kovera, M. B. (2019). Racial disparities in the criminal justice system: Prevalence, causes, and a search for solutions. *Journal of Social Issues*, *75*(4), 1139–1164. https://doi.org/10.1111/josi.12355

Ladson-Billings, G. (1994). What we can learn from multicultural education research. *Educational Leadership*, *51*(8), 22–26.

Ladson-Billings, G. (1995a). But that's just good teaching! The case for culturally relevant pedagogy. *Theory Into Practice*, *34*(3), 159–165. https://doi.org/10.1080/00405849509543675

Ladson-Billings, G. (1995b). Toward a theory of culturally relevant pedagogy. *American Educational Research Journal*, *32*(3), 465–491.

Ladson-Billings, G. (2000). Fighting for our lives. *Journal of Teacher Education*, *51*(3), 206–214. https://eric.ed.gov/?id=EJ613868

Ladson-Billings, G. (2014). Culturally Relevant Pedagogy 2.0: a.k.a. the Remix. *Harvard Educational Review*, *84*(1), 74–84.

Lara-Cinisomo, S., Fuligni, A., Daugherty, L., Howes, C., & Karoly, L. (Jan 26, 2009). A qualitative study of early childhood educators' beliefs about key preschool classroom experiences. RAND Working Paper No. WR- 656 (pp. 1–32). http://dx.doi.org/10.2139/ssrn.1333307

The Leadership Conference on Civil and Human Rights and The Leadership Conference Education Fund. (July 2022). *Holding the line: Combating racial discrimination in a divided America*. Author. https://civilrightsdocs.info/pdf/reports/CERD-report-Leadership-Conference-2022.pdf

Lee, D. M. (2012). *Creating an anti-racist classroom: Reflections to level the playing field*. Edutopia. https://www.edutopia.org/blog/anti-racist-classroom-danielle-moss-lee

Leech, T. G. J., Adams, E. A., Weathers, T. D., Staten, L. K., & Filippelli, G. M. (2016). Inequitable chronic lead exposure: A dual legacy of social and environmental injustice. *Family and Community Health*, *39*(3), 151–159. https://www.jstor.org/stable/48515477

Legette, K. B., Rogers, L. O., & Warren, C. A. (2022). Humanizing student-teacher relationships for black children: Implications for teachers' social–emotional training. *Urban Education*, *57*(2), 278–288. https://doi.org/10.1177/00420859 20933319

Little, B. & Hopkins, R. (2014). *Native Americans, boarding schools, and cultural genocide*. American Indian Resource Center, UC–Santa Cruz. https://airc.ucsc.edu/resources/schools-little.pdf

Lloyd, C. M., Carlson, J., Barnett, H., Shaw, S., & Logan, D. (2021). *Mary Pauper: A historical exploration of early care and education compensation, policy, and solutions*. Child Trends. https://earlyedcollaborative.org/assets/2022/04/Mary-Pauper-updated-4_4_2022_FINAL.pdf

Lopez, I. F. K. (1995). The social construction of race. In R. Delgado (Ed.), *Critical race theory: The cutting edge* (pp. 191–202). Temple University Press.

Love, B. L. (2019). *We want to do more than survive: Abolitionist teaching and the pursuit of educational freedom*. Beacon Press.

Lugo-Gil, J., Sattar, S., Ross, C., Boller, K., Tout, K., & Kirby, G. (2011). *The Quality Rating and Improvement System (QRIS) evaluation toolkit* (OPRE Report

#2011-31). U.S. Department of Health and Human Services, Administration for Children and Families, Office of Planning, Research and Evaluation.

Lund, D. E., & Lee, L. (2015). Fostering cultural humility among pre-service teachers: Connecting with child and youth of immigrant families through service learning. *Canadian Journal of Education, 38*(2), 1–30.

Macrae, T., Hoge, R., & Farquharson, K. (2022). Consonant cluster productions in preschool children who speak African American English. *Journal of Speech, Language, and Hearing Research, 65*(4), 1370–1385.

Mader, J. (2020). *Experts answer your kids' tough questions about race and racism: What to say when your child asks why police are mean to Black people, and other questions.* The Hechinger Report. https://hechingerreport.org/experts-answer-your-kids-tough-questions-about-race-and-racism/

Manning, M., Wong, G. T., Fleming, C. M., & Garvis, S. (2019). Is teacher qualification associated with the quality of the early childhood education and care environment? A meta-analytic review. *Review of Educational Research, 89*(3), 370–415.

Mapping Police Violence. (2022). *Resources.* https://mappingpoliceviolence.org/resources

Mayes, R. D., Pianta, R., Oglesby, A., & Zyromski, B. (2022). Principles of anti-racist social emotional justice learning. *Theory Into Practice, 61*(2), 178–187. https://doi.org/10.1080/00405841.2022.2036063

McLean, C., Austin, L. J. E., Whitebook, M., & Olson, K. L. (2021). *Early Childhood Workforce Index 2020.* Center for the Study of Child Care Employment, University of California—Berkeley. https://cscce.berkeley.edu/workforce-index-2020/report-pdf/

McNeal, L. R. (2009). The re-segregation of public education now and after the end of Brown v. Board of Education. *Education and Urban Society, 41*(5), 562–574. https://doi.org/10.1177/0013124509333578

Meek, S., Iruka, I. U., Allen, R., Yazzie, D., Fernandez, V., Catherine, E., McIntosh, K., Gordon, L., Gilliam, W., Hemmeter, M. L., Blevins, D., & Powell, T. (2020). *Start with equity: Fourteen priorities to dismantle systemic racism in early care and education.* Center for Child and Family Success, Arizona State University. https://childandfamilysuccess.asu.edu/cep/initiatives/start-with-equity-14-priorities-dismantle-systemic-racism-early-care-education

Meek, S., Iruka, I. U., Soto-Boykin, X., Blevins, D., Alexander, B., Cardona, M., & Castro, D. (2022). *Equity is quality, quality is equity: Operationalizing equity in quality rating and improvement systems.* Center for Child and Family Success, Arizona State University. https://childandfamilysuccess.asu.edu/sites/default/files/2022-06/QRIS-report-061722 (3).pdf

Mendoza, V. (2001). They came to Kansas searching for a better life. In J. M. Hawes & E. I. Nybakken (Eds.), *Family & society in American history* (pp. 215–225). University of Illinois Press.

Michel, S. (2012). The History of Childcare in the U.S. Retrieved January 30, 2023 from: https://socialwelfare.library.vcu.edu/programs/child-care-the-american-history/.

Mikati, I., Benson, A. F., Luben, T. J., Sacks, J. D., & Richmond-Bryant, J. (2018). Disparities in distribution of particulate matter emission sources by race and

poverty status. *American Journal of Public Health*, *108*(4), 480–485. https://doi
.org/10.2105/AJPH.2017.304297

Miller, S. (2019). *Don't touch my hair!* Little, Brown & Company.

Morrow, L. M. (1990). Preparing the classroom environment to promote literacy
during play. *Early Childhood Research Quarterly*, *5*(4), 537–554. https://doi
.org/10.1016/0885-2006(90)90018-v

Morrow, L. M., & Rand, M. K. (1991). Promoting literacy during play by designing
early childhood classroom environments. *The Reading Teacher*, *44*(6), 396–402.
https://www.jstor.org/stable/20200675

Muñiz, J. (2020). *Culturally responsive teaching: A reflection guide*. New America.

Musu-Gillette, L., De Brey, C., McFarland, J., Hussar, W., Sonnenberg, W., &
Wilkinson-Flicker, S. (2017). Status and Trends in the Education of Racial and
Ethnic Groups 2017. NCES 2017-051. *National Center for Education Statistics*.

NAACP. (n.d.). *The origins of modern day policing: Slave patrols*. https://naacp.org
/find-resources/history-explained/origins-modern-day-policing

NAEYC. (2019). *Professional standards and competencies for early childhood educators* [Position statement]. https://www.naeyc.org/resources/position-statements
/professional-standards-competencies

NAEYC. (2020a). *Developmentally appropriate practice* [Position statement].
https://www.naeyc.org/sites/default/files/globally-shared/downloads/PDFs
/resources/position-statements/dap-statement_0.pdf

NAEYC (2020b). *Unifying Framework for the Early Childhood Education Profession*. Retrieved January 30, 2023 from http://powertotheprofession.org/wp
-content/uploads/2020/03/Press-Release_Unifying-Framework.pdf.

National Academies of Sciences, Engineering, and Medicine [NASEM]. (2019). *Vibrant
and healthy kids: Aligning science, practice, and policy to advance health equity*.
The National Academies Press. https://doi.org/https://doi.org/10.17226/25466

National Congress of American Indians (2020). *Tribal Nations & the United States:
An introduction*. https://www.ncai.org/about-tribes

Neblett, E. W., Jr. (2019). Racism and health: Challenges and future directions in
behavioral and psychological research. *Cultural Diversity and Ethnic Minority
Psychology*, *25*(1), 12–20. https://doi.org/10.1037/cdp0000253

Neblett, E. W., Jr., Philip, C. L., Cogburn, C. D., & Sellers, R. M. (2006). African
American adolescents' discrimination experiences and academic achievement:
Racial socialization as a cultural compensatory and protective factor. *Journal of
Black Psychology*, *32*(2), 199–218.

Nellis, A., Liston, S., & En, S. (2021). *The color of justice: Racial and ethnic disparity in state prisons*. The Sentencing Project. https://www.sentencingproject.org
/wp-content/uploads/2016/06/The-Color-of-Justice-Racial-and-Ethnic
-Disparity-in-State-Prisons.pdf

Newheiser, A.-K., & Olson, K. (2012). White and Black American children's implicit
intergroup bias. *Journal of Experimental Social Psychology*, *48*(1), 264–270.

Nzewi, K., Ignatius, M., & Kruckle, K. (2020). *Quality Improvement in California*.
California Child Care Resource & Referral Network. https://rrnetwork.org
/assets/general-files/Master-Plan-QRIS.pdf

Office for Civil Rights. (2021). *An overview of exclusionary discipline practices in
public schools for the 2017–18 school year*. U. S. Department of Education,

Civil Rights ata Collection. https://www2.ed.gov/about/offices/list/ocr/docs/crdc
-exclusionary-school-discipline.pdf

Office of Head Start. (n.d.). *Head Start Program performance standards, Sect. 1302.91: Staff qualifications and competency requirements.* U.S. Department of Health and Human Services, Administration for Children and Families, Head Start Early Childhood Learning & Knowledge Center. https://eclkc.ohs.acf.hhs.gov/policy/45-cfr-chap-xiii/1302-91-staff-qualifications-competency-requirements

Orfield, G., Frankenberg, E., Ee, J., & Kuscera, J. (2014). *Brown at 60: Great progress, a long retreat and an uncertain future.* Civil Rights Project. https://civilrightsproject.ucla.edu/research/k-12-education/integration-and-diversity/brown-at-60-great-progress-a-long-retreat-and-an-uncertain-future

Orfield, G., & Jarvie, D. (2020). *Black segregation matters: School resegregation and Black educational opportunity.* UCLA Civil Rights Project. https://www.civilrightsproject.ucla.edu/research/k-12-education/integration-and-diversity/black-segregation-matters-school-resegregation-and-black-educational-opportunity/BLACK-SEGREGATION-MATTERS-final-121820.pdf

Osta, K., & Vasquez, H. (2019). *Don't talk about implicit bias without talking about structural racism.* National Equity Project. https://medium.com/national-equity-project/implicit-bias-structural-racism-6c52cf0f4a92

Page, N., & Czuba, C. E. (1999). Empowerment: What is it? *Journal of Extension, 37*(5), 1-5.2.367

Pager, D., & Western, B. (2012). Identifying discrimination at work: The use of field experiments. *Journal of Social Issues, 68*(2), 221–237. https://doi.org/10.1111/j.1540-4560.2012.01746.x

Papadopoulos, A. (2021). The world's most powerful countries for 2021, ranked. *CEOWorld Magazine.* https://ceoworld.biz/2021/01/02/the-worlds-most-powerful-countries-for-2021-ranked/

Parks, V. (2016). Rosa Parks redux: Racial mobility projects on the journey to work. *Annals of the American Association of Geographers, 106*(2), 292–299. https://doi.org/10.1080/00045608.2015.1100061

Peters, M. F. (1985). Racial socialization of young Black children. In H. P. McAdoo & J. L. McAdoo (Eds.), *Black children: Social, educational, and parental environments* (pp. 159-173). Sage.

Peters, S. J., Matthews, M. S., McBee, M. T., & McCoach, D. B. (2021). *Beyond gifted education: Designing and implementing advanced academic programs.* Routledge.

Petersen, E. E., Davis, N. L., Goodman, D., Cox, S., Syverson, C., Seed, K., Shapiro-Mendoza, C., Callaghan, W. M., & Barfield, W. (2019, September). Racial/ethnic disparities in pregnancy-related deaths—United States, 2007–2016. *Morbidity and Mortality Weekly Report, 68*(35), 762–765. https://www.cdc.gov/mmwr/volumes/68/wr/mm6835a3.htm

Pew Research Center. (2015). Use of spanking differs across racial and education groups. https://www.pewresearch.org/social-trends/2015/12/17/parenting-in-america/st_2015-12-17_parenting-09/

Pierce, K., Carter, C., Weinfeld, M., Desmond, J., Hazin, R., Bjork, R., & Gallagher, N. (2011). Detecting, Studying, and Treating Autism Early: The One-Year Well-Baby Check-Up Approach. *The Journal of Pediatrics, 159*(3), 458–465.e456. https://doi.org/10.1016/j.jpeds.2011.02.036

Porter, T., Bromer, J., & Moodie, S. (2011). *Quality Rating and Improvement Systems (QRIS) and family-sensitive caregiving in early care and education arrangements: Promising directions and challenges* (Issue Brief OPRE 2011-11d). Office of Planning, Research and Evaluation, Administration for Children and Families, U.S. Department of Health and Human Services. https://www.acf.hhs.gov/sites/default/files/documents/opre/qrisfsc_0.pdf

Power to the Profession. (2020). *Unifying framework for the early childhood education profession: Executive summary.* http://powertotheprofession.org/wp-content/uploads/2020/03/Power-to-Profession-Framework-exec-summary-03082020.pdf

Rashid, H. M. (2009). From brilliant baby to child placed at risk: The perilous path of African American boys in early childhood education. *The Journal of Negro Education, 78*(3), 347–358.

Ray, R., Perry, A. M., Harshbarger, D., Elizondo, S., & Gibbons, A. (2021). *Homeownership, racial segregation, and policy solutions to racial wealth equity.* Brookings. https://www.brookings.edu/essay/homeownership-racial-segregation-and-policies-for-racial-wealth-equity/

Reyes, M. R., Brackett, M. A., Rivers, S. E., White, M., & Salovey, P. (2012). Classroom emotional climate, student engagement, and academic achievement. *Journal of Educational Psychology, 104*(3), 700–712. https://doi.org/10.1037/a0027268

Richmond-Bryant, J., Mikati, I., Benson, A. F., Luben, T. J., & Sacks, J. D. (2020). Disparities in distribution of particulate matter emissions from US coal-fired power plants by race and poverty status after accounting for reductions in operations between 2015 and 2017. *American Journal of Public Health, 110*(5), 655–661. https://doi.org/10.2105/AJPH.2019.305558

Rivas-Drake, D., Lozada, F. T., Pinetta, B. J., & Jagers, R. J. (2020). School-based social-emotional learning and ethnic-racial identity among African American and Latino adolescents. *Youth & Society, 52*(7), 1331–1354. https://doi.org/10.1177/0044118x20939736

Rodgers, W. M., III. (2022, July 4). Reducing racial employment gaps for young adults without college education. Federal Reserve Bank of St. Louis, *On the Economy.* https://www.stlouisfed.org/on-the-economy/2022/may/racial-employment-gaps-young-adults-without-college

Rosado, A., Cohn-Postar, G., & Eisen, M. (2022). *Erasing the Black freedom struggle: How state standards fail to teach the truth about Reconstruction.* Zinn Education Project. https://www.teachreconstructionreport.org

Ross, T. (1990). The rhetorical tapestry of race: White innocence and Black abstraction. *William & Mary Law Review, 32*(1), 1–40.

Rucinski, C. L., Brown, J. L., & Downer, J. T. (2018). Teacher–child relationships, classroom climate, and children's social-emotional and academic development. *Journal of Educational Psychology, 110*(7), 992–1004. https://doi.org/10.1037/edu0000240

Sabol, T. J., Hong, S. S., Pianta, R. C., & Burchinal, M. R. (2013). Can rating pre-K programs predict children's learning? *Science, 341*(6148), 845–846.

Sampson, R. J., & Winter, A. S. (2016). The racial ecology of lead poisoning: Toxic inequality in Chicago neighborhoods, 1995–2013. *Du Bois Review: Social*

Science Research on Race, 13(2), 261–283. https://doi.org/10.1017/S1742058X 16000151

Sanders, M. G. (1997). Overcoming obstacles: Academic achievement as a response to racism and discrimination. *Journal of Negro Education, 66*(1), 83–93.

Schaeffer, K. (2021). *America's public school teachers are far less racially and ethnically diverse than their students.* Pew Research Center. https://www.pewresearch.org/fact-tank/2021/12/10/americas-public-school-teachers-are-far-less-racially-and-ethnically-diverse-than-their-students/

Scott-Clayton, J., & Li, J. (2016). *Black-white disparity in student loan debt more than triples after graduation* (Evidence Speaks Reports, 2(3)). Brookings Center on Children & Families. https://www.brookings.edu/wp-content/uploads/2016/10/es_20161020_scott-clayton_evidence_speaks.pdf

Scottham, K. M., Sellers, R. M., & Nguyên, H. X. (2008). A measure of racial identity in African American adolescents: The development of the Multidimensional Inventory of Black Identity—Teen. *Cultural Diversity and Ethnic Minority Psychology, 14*(4), 297–306. https://doi.org/10.1037/1099-9809.14.4.297

Seguin, C., & Rigby, D. (2019). National crimes: A new national data set of lynchings in the United States, 1883 to 1941. *Socius, 5.* https://doi.org/10.1177/2378023 119841780

Sellers, R. M., Smith, M. A., Shelton, J. N., Rowley, S. A. J., & Chavous, T. M. (1998). Multidimensional model of racial identity: A reconceptualization of African American racial identity. *Personality and Social Psychology Review, 2*(1), 18–39. https://doi.org/10.1207/s15327957pspr0201_2

Shockley, E. (2011). *Renegade poetics: Black aesthetics and formal innovation in African American poetry.* University of Iowa Press.

Shockley, K. G. (2009). A researcher 'called' to 'taboo' places?: A burgeoning research method in African-centered education. *International Journal of Qualitative Studies in Education, 22*(2), 163–176. https://doi.org/10.1080/09518390701706682

Simon, C. (2021). The role of race and ethnicity in parental ethnic-racial socialization: A scoping review of research. *Journal of Child and Family Studies, 30*(1), 182–195. https://doi.org/10.1007/s10826-020-01854-7

Sium, A., & Ritskes, E. (2013). Speaking truth to power: Indigenous storytelling as an act of living resistance. *Decolonization: Indigeneity, Education & Society, 2*(1), I–X.

Smith, C. (2017, September 11). *Persona dolls and anti-bias curriculum practice with young children: A case study of early childhood development teachers* [Doctoral dissertation, University of Capetown]. Academia.edu. https://www.academia.edu/en/34535115/Persona_Dolls_and_anti_bias_curriculum_practice_with _young_children_A_case_study_of_Early_Childhood_Development_teachers

Smithers, G. D. (2012). *Slave breeding: Sex, violence, and memory in African American history.* University Press of Florida.

Spaulding, E. C., Adams, J., Dunn, D. C., & Love, B. L. (2021). Freedom dreaming anti-racist pedagogy dreams. *Language Arts, 99*(1), 8–18.

Squires, J., Bricker, D. D., & Twombly, E. (2009). *Ages & stages questionnaires* (pp. 257–182). Paul H. Brookes.

Stearns, D. C. (2012). Janitors and maids. *Neurobics.* http://deborahstearns.blogspot.com/2012/07/janitors-and-maids.html

Stevenson, H. (2014). *Promoting racial literacy in schools: Differences that make a difference.* Teachers College Press.

Sun, J., Goforth, A. N., Nichols, L. M., Violante, A., Christopher, K., Howlett, R., Hogenson, D., & Graham, N. (2022). Building a space to dream: Supporting Indigenous children's survivance through community-engaged social and emotional learning. *Child Development, 93*(3), 699–716. https://doi.org/10.1111/cdev.13786

Tenenbaum, H. R., & Ruck, M. D. (2007). Are teachers' expectations different for racial minority than for European American students? A meta-analysis. *Journal of Educational Psychology, 99*(2), 253–273. https://doi.org/10.1037/0022-0663.99.2.253

Tervalon, M., & Murray-Garcia, J. (1998). Cultural humility versus cultural competence: A critical distinction in defining physician training outcomes in multicultural education. *Journal of Health Care for the Poor and Underserved, 9*(2), 117–125. https://doi.org/10.1353/hpu.2010.0233

Ullrich, R., Hamm, K., & Herzfeldt-Kamprath, R. (2016). Underpaid and unequal: Racial wage disparities in the early childhood workforce. https://www.americanprogress.org/wp-content/uploads/2016/08/NSECE-report2.pdf

U.S. Department of Health and Human Services, Administration for Children and Families, Office of Head Start. (2021). *Head Start Performance Standards: 45 CFR Chapter XIII.* Author. https://eclkc.ohs.acf.hhs.gov/sites/default/files/pdf/hspps-final.pdf

Vogtman, J. (2017). *Undervalued: A brief history of women's care work and child care policy in the United States.* National Women's Law Center. https://nwlc.org/wp-content/uploads/2017/12/final_nwlc_Undervalued2017.pdf

Walker, G. (March, 2020). Early Childhood Educators Establish Professional Standards, Guidelines, and Accountability, Call for Significant Increases in Public Investment. Retrieved January 30, 2023 from http://powertotheprofession.org/wp-content/uploads/2020/03/Press-Release_Unifying-Framework.pdf

Warren, C. A., Presberry, C., & Louis, L. (2022). Examining teacher dispositions for evidence of (transformative) social and emotional competencies with Black boys: The case of three urban high school teachers. *Urban Education, 57*(2), 251–277. https://doi.org/10.1177/0042085920933326

Washington, V. (Ed). (2019). *Child Development Associate Essentials Workbook* (2nd ed.). Council for Professional Recognition.

Webb, E., Maddocks, A., & Bongilli, J. (2002). Effectively protecting black and minority ethnic children from harm: overcoming barriers to the child protection process. *Child Abuse Review, 11*(6), 394–410. https://doi.org/https://doi.org/10.1002/car.760

Whitebook, M., McLean, C., Austin, L. J. E., & Edwards, B. (2018). *Early Childhood Workforce Index 2018.* Center for the Study of Child Care Employment, University of California–Berkeley. https://cscce.berkeley.edu/wp-content/uploads/2022/04/Early-Childhood-Workforce-Index-2018.pdfhttps://cscce.berkeley.edu/wp-content/uploads/2022/04/Early-Childhood-Workforce-Index-2018.pdf

The White House. (2021a, October 28). *The Build Back Better framework.* https://www.whitehouse.gov/briefing-room/statements-releases/2021/10/28/build-back-better-framework/

The White House. (2021b, April 28). *Fact sheet: The American Families Plan.* https://www.whitehouse.gov/briefing-room/statements-releases/2021/04/28/fact-sheet-the-american-families-plan/

Williams, B. V., & Jagers, R. J. (2022). Transformative social and emotional learning: Work notes on an action research agenda. *Urban Education, 57*(2), 191–197.

Wymer, S. C., Corbin, C. M., & Williford, A. P. (2022). The relation between teacher and child race, teacher perceptions of disruptive behavior, and exclusionary discipline in preschool. *Journal of School Psychology, 90,* 33–42.

Yosso, T. J. (2005). Whose culture has capital? A critical race theory discussion of community cultural wealth. *Race Ethnicity and Education, 8*(1), 69–91. https://doi.org/10.1080/1361332052000341006

Index

About the Authors

Iheoma U. Iruka (she/her/hers) is a research professor in public policy and the founding director of the Equity Research Action Coalition at the Frank Porter Graham Child Development Institute at The University of North Carolina at Chapel Hill.

Tonia R. Durden (she/her/hers) is a clinical professor and birth through five program coordinator in the Department of Early Childhood and Elementary Education at Georgia State University.

Kerry-Ann Escayg (she/her/hers) is an associate professor of teacher education at the University of Nebraska–Omaha.

Stephanie M. Curenton (she/her/hers) is a professor and director of the Center on the Ecology of Early Development program at Boston University.

LAND ACKNOWLEDGMENT

Dr. Iheoma U. Iruka. I acknowledge that I live, work, and build my family's economic wealth on Lumbee tribal land taken through colonization and attempted eradication by white settlers. The Lumbee Tribe is one of eight recognized tribes in North Carolina. The other tribes are the Coharie, the Eastern Band of Cherokee Indians, the Haliwa-Saponi, the Meherrin, the Sappony, the Occaneechi Band of the Saponi Nation, and the Waccamaw Siouan. The Lumbee Tribe provides programs and services to all tribal members within the areas of Cumberland, Hoke, Robeson, and Scotland Counties in North Carolina. I also acknowledge the Massa-adchu-es-et (Massachusetts) and Pawtucket tribes in Massachusetts where I grew up. It is critical to take a moment to acknowledge and honor the Indigenous inhabitants of the past and those who are still here and whose land we now live and create our wealth on. This land acknowledgment opens up greater consciousness about Native sovereignty, and more importantly, it begs us to ask ourselves how and why their land was taken; what forces were so strong as to drive others to take over large swaths of land where people were living, burying loved ones, and just living life. We must reflect on and honor their ancient knowledge and wisdom, which is still with us.

Dr. Tonia R. Durden. I was born and raised and currently work in Atlanta, Georgia. I would like to acknowledge that I have lived and worked on land that was stolen from the Muscogee (Creek) Nation. The Muscogee Nation were forcefully removed from their homes as the result of the Indian Removal Act and murdered while attempting to be neutral during the American Civil War. During the Reconstruction period, more Muscogee tribal land was stolen. It is important to take a moment to acknowledge the atrocities and acts of terrorism that was perpetuated against the Muscogee people. I also want to acknowledge and recognize their steadfastness, strength, and honorable tenacity in rebuilding and restructuring their government and pushing back (HARD) against attempts at stealing from them their right to become a sovereign nation. *Ashe* to the ancestors and people of the Muscogee Nation.

Dr. Kerry-Ann Escayg. Supporting Indigenous sovereignty and justice for Indigenous peoples is central to anti-racist work. Thus, I would like to acknowledge that I reside on the land of the Ponca Tribe, the Winnebago Tribe, and the Santee Sioux tribe. Despite the gross injustices of the past, Indigenous groups exemplify resistance and strength, drawing on ancestral wisdom, cultural knowledges, and practices to not only heal from colonial violence in its varied forms, but also to guide future generations in the revolutionary spirit of anticolonialism and decolonization. I stand in solidarity with you and honor your individual and collective resistance.

Dr. Stephanie M. Curenton. I acknowledge—and pay honor to—the Wampanoag People who nurtured and inhabited the land where I now reside in Canton, Massachusetts. Their ancestors lived and thrived for thousands of years before European settlers misappropriated the land in the 17th century. Before European settlements, the Wampanoag existed in a confederation of at least 24 recorded tribes with population sizes in the thousands, where women served as the keepers of the culture, the land, and the family. Although the tribes fought bravely against colonialism, the warfare and illness brought by the Europeans drastically decreased their population. My respect goes out to not only the Wampanoag ancestors, but also their descendants who continue to live and thrive on this land throughout New England and elsewhere.

I also acknowledge and pay honor to the Seneca tribe ruled by Queen Aliquippa in the Southwestern Pennsylvania lands surrounding the three rivers (Ohio, Allegheny, and Monongahela), which is the land of my birth and childhood. I am grateful to have been reared on land named after such a wise and powerful leader, and I pray that her spirit protects and guides me throughout my life as I strive to honor her memory and her land.

Go to the Native Land map at https://native-land.ca/ and identify what Native land you live on, grew up on, and work on. Once you discover the name of the Native tribes, think about what being on this land every day allows you to do. What if this was your land and someone took it away from you? Find out more about the tribes: if they are in existence, what are their cultural traditions, language, and history? How can you acknowledge them in your life (e.g., talk about it, share it with others, put it on your email signature, read more about them)?

BODY ACKNOWLEDGEMENT

Enslaved Africans and their enslaved descendants built many parts of the United States, and only within the past generation were Black people afforded full rights. Black individuals (and other people of color, including Mexicans, Native Americans, and Japanese) work as service staff across the country. This community is mainly responsible for maintaining our daily lives: food service available, early care and education, transportation, health care, and many other basic necessities that make our lives easy. The wealth of our nation is due to the forced free labor of these Africans and their descendants.

Printed and bound by CPI Group (UK) Ltd, Croydon, CR0 4YY

09/06/2025

14685970-0001